THE BRITISH ACADEMY

The
Septuagint and Jewish Worship
A Study in Origins

By

H. St. John Thackeray, M.A.
HON. D.D. OXFORD, HON. D.D. DURHAM

Some time Grinfield Lecturer on the Septuagint
in the University of Oxford

1869- 1930

The Schweich Lectures
1920

Wipf & Stock
PUBLISHERS
Eugene, Oregon

Wipf and Stock Publishers
199 W 8th Ave, Suite 3
Eugene, OR 97401

The Septuagint and Jewish Worship
By Thackeray, H. St. J.
ISBN 13: 978-1-55635-159-4
ISBN 10: 1-55635-159-3
Publication date 12/22/2006
Previously published by British Academy, 1921

TO THE MEMORY OF

HENRY BARCLAY SWETE

IN GRATEFUL RECOLLECTION

OF GUIDANCE AND INSPIRATION

IN SEPTUAGINT STUDIES

PREFACE

THIS book contains in an expanded form, with the addition of Appendices, the three Schweich Lectures for 1920 delivered last December. I have divided into two the second Lecture, which time did not permit of being delivered in full.

In doing me the honour to appoint me to the Schweich Lectureship, the British Academy kindly offered me the opportunity of putting together the results of my researches into the Septuagint. The subject which originally suggested itself to me was 'The liturgical use of the Old Testament as a factor in exegesis'; a subject which has not been worked out, as it deserves to be, and one on which the LXX supplies important, though not the only, evidence. This now forms the basis of Lectures II and III; in Lecture II, while keeping the LXX mainly in view, I ventured to digress a little beyond my proper province. The first lecture on Septuagint origins was prefixed under advice.

The Lectures are a combination of things new and old. The nucleus of I and II appeared in various contributions to the *Journal of Theological Studies*, to the editors and publishers of which I am indebted for permission to reprint portions of the Tables which stand in the Appendix. The Lectures themselves embody the results of a careful re-examination of the books concerned. Lecture III is wholly new. Here I have reluctantly retracted opinions previously expressed and I cannot claim to have said the last word on the Book of Baruch; but I hope that the main idea (the liturgical framework, strangely overlooked by the commentators) may prove to be sound.

I have also to express my thanks to kind friends at Oxford, to whom I am otherwise so deeply indebted, for permitting me to make use of the materials of my Grinfield lectures delivered some years ago.

H. ST. J. THACKERAY.

MARSHAM LANE HOUSE, GERRARD'S CROSS,
   St. Mark's Day, 1921.

CONTENTS

LECTURE I.

SKETCH OF SEPTUAGINT ORIGINS:

THE TRANSLATORS OF THE PROPHETICAL BOOKS

LECTURE II

THE SEPTUAGINT AND JEWISH WORSHIP:

(1) THE FEAST OF PENTECOST

LECTURE II *(continued)*

THE SEPTUAGINT AND JEWISH WORSHIP:

(2) THE FEAST OF TABERNACLES

LECTURE III

THE SEPTUAGINT AND JEWISH WORSHIP:

(3) The Book of Baruch and the Fast of the Ninth Ab

APPENDICES

LECTURE I

SKETCH OF SEPTUAGINT ORIGINS:

The Translators of the Prophetical Books

I HAVE had the honour of being invited by the British Academy to put before you some results of my researches into the oldest translation of the Hebrew Bible, the Alexandrian Greek version commonly known as the Septuagint. The Septuagint has many claims on our attention. By diffusing for the first time a knowledge of the Hebrew Scriptures to the world at large it was a *Praeparatio Evangelica* paving the way for Christianity; it was the Bible of the early Church and the parent of numerous daughter versions. Its language is a mine of information on Κοινή Greek, the *lingua franca* of the new era dating from Alexander the Great. But, over and above these and other subsidiary interests, its main importance consists in its being a translation of a Hebrew text older by a millennium than our earliest dated Hebrew MS.; and, in particular, older by a few centuries than the rabbinical revision of the original which took place about A.D. 100. Crude and illiterate as it often is, the production of men who, labouring under grave difficulties, not infrequently misread and blundered over the Hebrew before them; with many imperfections, and transmitted in a text which has itself suffered serious corruption, the LXX nevertheless supplies the patient investigator, from time to time, with the materials for the reconstruction of an older Hebrew than that represented in our modern Bibles.

I have called my lectures 'a study in origins'. Under origins I include the beginnings both of the LXX and of Jewish worship; the two, I believe, are intimately connected. To-day I propose to give a sketch of LXX origins, in so far as tradition and the work itself enable us to reconstruct the history; and to attempt, in the case of two selected portions, to investigate the methods of the translators and to account for the form in which their work has come down to us. The remaining lectures will hinge upon Jewish worship. In Lecture II I shall consider how far the use of portions of Scripture in public worship has left its mark upon the text; touching on the origins of the festival services and the yet more remote origins of the festivals. In Lecture III I shall apply this line of inquiry to a single book, the whole structure of which seems to be governed by what I may call the 'liturgical' motive.

I may begin by briefly recapitulating the three main stages in the rather complex early history of the Greek text. We have first the original Alexandrian translations dating from the third to the first century B.C.; next the rival versions of the Asiatic school in the second century of our era, and last the unavailing efforts of Origen in the next century to establish a uniform text by a fusion of the work of these two schools.

'Always something new from Africa', says the proverb, and perhaps even the land of the Pyramids never produced a novelty which had a profounder and more enduring influence than the Greek Bible. Long before the foundation of the great city on the western arm of the Delta, Egypt had possessed the nucleus of a Jewish colony. When Jeremiah was dragged thither against his will, we read of Jews settled 'at Migdol, and at Tahpanhes, and at Noph, and in the country of Pathros'.[1] And it is only in recent years that we have learnt of the outlying colony living as early as the sixth century B.C. far up the Nile at Elephantine. But it was the expedition of Alexander and the founding of Alexandria in 332 B.C. which marked the beginning of a new era for the Egyptian 'dispersion'. If Alexander's ambitious scheme of a world-empire ended, like similar latter-day schemes, in failure, his meteoric career had one enduring and beneficent effect, that of diffusing a knowledge of the Greek language and culture throughout a large portion of the eastern world. Lower Egypt, in particular, fostered the use of this international tongue, and Alexandria became not only the University of Greek learning, but the world's market and centre of commerce with Greek as the medium for all business transactions.

Among the colonists of the new city the Jews formed no inconsiderable element. Befriended by Alexander, they were rewarded for their services in his army by the gift of full citizenship and a quarter of their own in Alexandria. So rapidly did the colony grow that by the beginning of our era the

[1] Jer. xliv. 1.

Egyptian Jews numbered a million [1] or an eighth part of the population of the country.

There can be little doubt that it was the religious needs of this thriving community which stimulated the ambitious project of translating the Scriptures. Hebrew, even in the home-land, had long since become a learned language; but in Egypt even the Aramaic paraphrase which served the needs of the Palestinian synagogues, had, at least to the second or third generation of immigrants, ceased to be intelligible. Clinging tenaciously to their faith, but driven by circumstances to abandon the use of Aramaic, this enterprising colony determined that their Law should be read in a language 'understanded of the people'. The Greek Bible, it seems, owed its origin to a popular demand for a version in the vulgar tongue.

It must be admitted that this is not the motive assigned by ancient tradition. Tradition, not content with so humble, if pious, an origin, must needs ascribe the work to the injunctions of royalty. I need not dwell on the familiar story, told in the so-called *Letter of Aristeas*, how Ptolemy Philadelphus, at the instance of his librarian Demetrius, summoned from Jerusalem seventy-two learned men to translate the Law, in order to fill a gap in the royal collection. Long since discredited as a contemporary and authentic narrative, there probably lies behind the romantic and apologetic framework some element of truth; though it is hard to disentangle fact from fiction. The original story is comparatively sober. The translators, we are told, collaborated and 'arrived at agreement on each point by comparing each other's work' (§ 302); the procedure described is quite natural and non-miraculous. It is only later writers who introduce miracle, asserting that the translators worked independently in separate cells or in pairs in thirty-six cells and all produced identical versions; that they translated the whole of the Scriptures, not only the Law; that they were no less inspired than the original authors, and so on.

In the original story I should, in general agreement with the late Dr. Swete, regard the following items as credible. (1) The Pentateuch forms a separate *corpus* within the Greek Bible. It was rendered first and, in view of its homogeneous style, as a whole. (2) The version is Alexandrian; it contains Egyptian words and the Egyptian papyri furnish the closest parallels to its language. (3) It goes well back into the third century B.C.;

---

[1] Philo, *In Flaccum*, 6 (43 Cohn).

the Greek Genesis and Exodus are cited before the end of the century,[1] and the style is akin to that of our earliest papyri. (4) It was the work of a company, probably a small company. The traditional number (seventy or seventy-two) is legendary; the alternative number, five, found in a Rabbinic version of the story,[2] is more likely to be true. (5) The Hebrew rolls may have been imported from Palestine. (6) Lastly, it is conceivable that the work was countenanced by Philadelphus, a patron of litera- ture and interested in the antiquities of his subjects. It was in his reign, and perhaps at his commission, that Manetho produced a Greek version of the records of ancient Egypt.[3] But that the work owed its inception wholly to him and his librarian is incredible. The Greek is the vernacular, that of the non-literary papyri, not the more cultivated style proper to a work produced under royal patronage. The importation of translators from Palestine is another fabrication; language proves them to have been indigenous. As the late Dr. Swete acutely observed, 'Aristeas' in stating that the translation was read to and approved by the community *before* being submitted to the king,[4] unconsciously throws light on its true origin. It was a people's book designed, undoubtedly, for synagogue use.

The origin of the traditional number of the translators and of their miraculous agreement in the later accounts has been traced in the LXX itself, in the narrative of the law-giving.[5] We there read of seventy elders who form a link between Moses and the people. They ascend the mount but a little way and worship from afar. Jewish fancy seems to have identified these mysterious elders with the translators, the intermediaries between Moses and Israel of the dispersion. The Greek states (*v.* 11) that not one of them perished, i. e. they were privileged to escape the usual death-penalty for a vision of the deity. But the verb used for 'perish' ($\delta\iota\alpha\phi\omega\nu\epsilon\hat{\iota}\nu$) was unusual in that sense; 'not one dis- agreed' was the more obvious meaning. Hence, it seems, arose the legend of the translators' supernatural agreement. Hence too, from their supposed presence on Sinai, the belief that they shared the lawgiver's inspiration.

The Greek Bible of the third century B. C. comprised only the Law. The translation of Prophets and 'Writings' followed in

[1] By the historian Demetrius; Swete, *Introd. to O. T.*[2], pp. 18, 369 f.

[2] *Masseketh Sopherim*, i. 8 (ed. J. Müller, 1878).

[3] Mahaffy, *Empire of the Ptolemies*, 170.

[4] Aristeas, § 308.

[5] Ex. xxiv. See Nestle in Hastings, *D. B.* iv. 439 a.

the course of the next two centuries. The evidence to be put before you to-day will throw light on the manner in which the Prophetical collection came into being. We shall find indications of the existence of a second company, analogous to the pioneering body responsible for the Greek Pentateuch. This second instalment was also, it seems, in large measure, a semi-official production.

Very different was the treatment of the Writings or Hagiographa. These stood on a lower level than Law and Prophets, being regarded as national literature, but not yet as canonical. The Psalter, at the head, was the one book in this category which the translators treated with respect. They appended, indeed, an additional Psalm, but expressly placed it 'outside the number'. The other books they did not scruple to handle freely, undeterred by any fear of tampering with Scripture. These paraphrases (rather than translations) were the outcome of individual enterprise. A partial rendering of Job (one sixth being omitted) was probably among the first; later on Theodotion's version was used to fill the gaps, and our Greek text is a conglomerate of old and new. The first Greek narrative of the return from exile (1 Esdras) was a similar version of extracts, grouped round a fable of heathen origin. The translator of these extracts appears responsible also for the earliest version of Daniel, which he treated similarly, again incorporating extraneous matter. The Greek Proverbs include maxims of purely Greek origin. The translator was a classical scholar and, happily, put much of his work into verse. Tags of rough hexameters and iambics abound. In Greek, as in most languages, proverbs commonly took the form of a rough line or half-line of verse. So 'Cold water to a thirsty soul' (xxv. 25) becomes

$$\ddot{\omega}\sigma\pi\epsilon\rho\ \ddot{\upsilon}\delta\omega\rho\ \psi\upsilon\chi\rho\grave{o}\nu\ \psi\upsilon\chi\tilde{\eta}\ \delta\iota\psi\acute{\omega}\sigma\eta\ \pi\rho\sigma\eta\nu\acute{\epsilon}s,$$

the first and last words being added to round off the hexameter, while the answering clause, if we add a final word, forms a second :

$$o\ddot{\upsilon}\tau\omega s\ \dot{\alpha}\gamma\gamma\epsilon\lambda\acute{\iota}\alpha\ \dot{\alpha}\gamma\alpha\theta\grave{\eta}\ \,\text{'}\kappa\ \gamma\tilde{\eta}s\ \mu\alpha\kappa\rho\acute{o}\theta\epsilon\nu\ \langle\ddot{\eta}\kappa\epsilon\iota\rangle.$$

Similarly in iambics we have $\pi\eta\gamma\grave{\eta}\ \zeta\langle o\rangle\tilde{\eta}s\ \ddot{\epsilon}\nu\nu o\iota\alpha\ \tau o\tilde{\iota}s\ \kappa\epsilon\kappa\tau\eta\mu\acute{\epsilon}\nu o\iota s$ (xvi. 22) and many others.[1]

Thus, it seems, was the Alexandrian Bible gradually built up. The second stage in the history begins towards the end of the first century of our era. It is a period of Palestinian revolt against the laxity and inadequacy of the Alexandrian versions.

[1] I may refer to my article on 'The Poetry of the Greek Book of Proverbs' in *J. T. S.* vol. xiii (1912), 46 ff.

At the first even the Palestinians had given the LXX a friendly reception. It was as freely used by Josephus as by the first converts to Christianity. Greek, according to Rabbi Simon ben Gamaliel, was the one language, beside Hebrew, in which the Scriptures might be written.[1] Soon, however, the work came to be viewed by the orthodox with suspicion. The reputed date of the original translation, observed at Alexandria as a feast-day,[2] was now kept by the Palestinians as a fast; and tradition asserted that the impious venture was punished by one of the old plagues of Egypt.[3] This revulsion of feeling was stimulated by two main causes: (1) the revision of the Hebrew text by R. Akiba and his school which took place about A.D. 100; (2) animosity against the wicked Christians who had appropriated and, as was alleged, distorted the LXX for their own ends. The Dispersion still, however, needed a Greek Bible, and the demand for greater accuracy and a stricter adherence to the revised Hebrew created an outburst of new translations. We know the names of three of these translators and possess considerable fragments of their work. The tendency to literalism culminated in the jargon of Aquila of Pontus, who, not from ignorance of Greek, but from a pedantic desire to present an exact reflex of every jot and tittle in the Hebrew, produced what has been called 'a colossal crib'.[4] The work of Theodotion of Ephesus was little more than a revision of the LXX or of other lost versions. A successful plagiarist, he is best known for his habit of transliteration, in other words for the evasion of the translator's function. Towards the end of the century comes Symmachus, whose elegant style reads like a direct challenge to Aquila's monstrosities. Since Asia was the home of two of these translators and perhaps of the third,[5] while Palestine supplied their text and canons of interpretation, we may call this the Asiatic-Palestinian school.

The third land-mark in the history is the *opus magnum* of the most eminent LXX scholar of antiquity, the *Hexapla* of Origen

---

[1] T. B. *Megillah*, i. 8 (quoted by Bentwich, *Hellenism*, 253).

[2] Philo, *Vit. Mos.* ii. 7 (41).

[3] 'On the 8th of Tebeth the Law was written in Greek in the days of King Tolmai, and darkness came upon the world for three days', Appendix to *Megillath Ta'anith* (ed. Neubauer, *Anecdota Oxon.*, Semitic Series, vol. i, pt. vi, Oxford, 1895).

[4] Burkitt in *J. Q. R.* Jan. 1898, p. 215.

[5] The scene of the only recorded incident in the life of Symmachus is Cappadocia.

of Alexandria. Designed to bring the LXX into line with the
revised Hebrew by the aid of the Asiatic translations, it exhibited
in parallel columns the Hebrew, the same in Greek letters, the
three later versions, and the LXX. The basis of the LXX
column was the current Alexandrian text of the third century;
this was supplemented or corrected where necessary by the later
versions, the interpolated matter being indicated by asterisks.
Origen's ambitious scheme was planned on faulty principles and
ultimately produced only confusion. Copies of the LXX column
were multiplied lacking the precautionary signs, and the resultant
mixture of old and new, of Alexandrian and Asiatic work, has
affected the mass of our MSS. The corruption of text, which
had begun before Origen's time, proceeded apace, and different
localities had their rival recensions. In the fourth century
three such recensions held the field, the so-called Hesychian
in Egypt, the Lucianic in Asia and Syria, the Hexaplaric in
Palestine; and, in Jerome's words, 'the whole world was divided
between these three varieties of text'.[1] At this period our oldest
Greek MS., the Codex Vaticanus, makes its appearance.

This brief sketch of some rather familiar history will show
that the reconstruction of the original Alexandrian version is
no easy task. Patient investigation of the style may, however,
enable us to distinguish, if I am not mistaken, not only between
the respective contributions of Egypt and Asia, but even, to
some extent, between the work of two or more primitive and
contemporary translators. The detection and elimination of
isolated glosses or 'doublets' is comparatively simple; larger
results may be looked for if the inquiry is spread over a wider
area. A study of the language, in fact, reveals *strata* in the
Greek Bible, such as are found in the Hebrew. Critics of the
Hebrew Pentateuch have reached certain generally received
conclusions as to its structure and component elements. The
primitive narratives of Jehovist and Elohist are followed some
centuries later by the Code of the Deuteronomist, and that again
by the Priestly document, forming the framework of the whole.
Methods which have proved efficacious in the larger task may
also assist the LXX critic to determine approximately the limits
of the work of the several translators. The various renderings
of divine titles like 'Lord of Hosts' have their tale to tell no less

---

[1] 'Totus ... orbis hac inter se trifaria varietate compugnat,' *Praef. in
Paralipp.*

than the use of Jahweh or Elohim in the original. Though we are far from the time when a Polychrome LXX will be possible, the student is now equipped with abundant materials for the investigation. Two results are possible. If I may borrow and distort the meaning of the symbols used by the critics of the Hebrew text, we may on the one hand discover that two primitive translators of the second century B. C., J and E, have produced of any particular book a joint version, JE, the symbols here standing for the Jewish-Egyptian pioneers. Or again, we may find that the original version JE (the work whether of one or more translators) was incomplete, and that it was left to P, a representative of the later Palestinian-Asiatic school, to fill the gaps and revise the whole. To-day I propose to put before you an instance of both types. My illustration of the completion in Asia of the unfinished work of Alexandria will be taken from the Books of Samuel and Kings; that of co-operation of contemporaries from Jeremiah, Ezekiel, and the Twelve.

The Books of Reigns

I take first, then, the Greek version of Samuel and Kings. Here we have, I believe, an instance of translation in two stages: a primitive partial rendering and a filling in of *lacunae* by a representative of the later school. Direct external evidence fails us; the evidence of style suggests that the conditions are the same as in the Greek book of Job. Here, moreover, we can account for the reserve of the earlier translators; patriotic concern for their nation's honour led them to produce an expurgated version of the history of the monarchy.

A word as to the *text* which is to serve as our guide. We have in these books three main types: (1) that represented by Codex Vaticanus (B) and printed in Dr. Swete's edition; (2) that of Codex Alexandrinus (A) the readings of which are recorded in his apparatus, and (3) the Lucianic recension, edited by Lagarde. Of these I follow the B text, though indeed my theory largely rests on readings on which all MSS. are agreed. The A text, obviously a mosaic, is negligible. Broadly speaking, it is a recension of the shorter B text, to bring it into line with the revised Hebrew; the additional matter, absent from B, being supplied mainly from Aquila, whose peculiarities are unmistakable. The only serious rival to B is the Lucianic text. This too, as will appear, has its contribution to yield; but, while it undoubtedly contains an ancient element, it also bears clear marks of editorial revision, and the more homogeneous and less eclectic B text, notwithstanding many shortcomings, forms a safer basis for our inquiry.

Titles and division of books first call for remark. In our Hebrew MSS. the history of the Monarchy is comprised in two undivided books with distinct titles—the Book of Samuel and the Book of Kings. In the LXX we have a single work entitled Βασιλειῶν in the four familiar volumes of our English Bible. While the translators have ultimately carried subdivision further than the Palestinians, the comprehensive title suggests that the narrative of the Monarchy may once have formed a unit with no division whatever. This is further suggested by the fact that the Greek MSS. differ as to the line of demarcation between the second and third books. On the Greek title two remarks may be made. Whatever its precise meaning, it is more appropriate than the first of the Hebrew titles; Samuel, whose judgeship occupies a comparatively small space, hardly deserves to give his name to the narrative of the reigns of Saul and David. Again, the title is not Kings, but Βασιλειῶν. As with the Book of Judges, which Philo calls the Book of Judgements (Κρίματα),[1] the Alexandrians preferred an impersonal to a personal title. What did they mean by the word? The usual rendering 'Kingdoms', if understood to refer to the twin kingdoms of Judah and Israel, will be another instance, like 'Samuel', of the part giving a name to the whole, since the disruption of the kingdom is not reached until nearly half-way through the third volume. In Hellenistic Greek, however, Βασιλεῖαι had another meaning, 'Reigns', and that, I believe, was the sense intended by the translators.

Now, on investigation, we find that the narrative falls into two main portions, one of which is characterized by certain mannerisms of the Asiatic school, while the other lacks these mannerisms and exhibits features peculiar to itself. I venture, therefore, to call these main groups the early and late portions. The 'late' matter is broken in two by intervening 'early' matter but is apparently the work of a single translator. The 'early' matter is divisible into three smaller volumes, which may or may not be the production of separate translators. Probably they are the work of a company; but stress cannot be laid on such minor differences of style as exist. The early portions are :—

Book I (1 Sam.). The Reign of Saul with preliminary events.

[1] *De Confus. Ling.* 26 (128 Wendland).

B

Book II (2 Sam. to xi. 1, stopping short of the Uriah episode).
The Reign of David in his prime.

Book III (1 Kings beginning at ii. 12, Solomon's accession,
and probably lacking the last chapter). The Reign of
Solomon and the beginnings of the Divided Monarchy.

That was the extent of the Alexandrian version. The two late
portions, by a single translator, are:—

(i) The last fourteen chapters of *Βασ.* II with the opening of
III, comprising David's sin and the disastrous sequel:
the tragic story of Tamar and Amnon, the rebellion and
death of Absalom, the revolt of Sheba, Adonijah's bid
for the succession and David's death.

(ii) The last chapter of *Βασ.* III with the whole of IV,
describing the growing degeneracy of the kings of Israel
and Judah, leading up to the double captivity.

My belief is that these two portions, which might collectively be
entitled 'The Decline and Fall of the Monarchy', were omitted
as unedifying by the early translators, or at least that they were
content with so brief a summary that it had subsequently to be
superseded by a complete version.[1]

The two new dividing-lines to be noted are those which mark
the beginning and end of the first instalment of the later work,
David's sin and David's death (2 R. xi. 2 and 3 R. ii. 11). We
have some other evidence, apart from that of style, for the narrative
being broken at these two points.

For the 'whitewashing' of David by the omission of discreditable
and disastrous incidents two illustrations can be quoted. In the
M.T. of 1 Kings (3 R.) xv. 3 ff. Abijam son of Rehoboam is con-
trasted with David. 'His heart', we read, 'was not perfect with
the LORD his God, as the heart of David his father. Nevertheless
for David's sake did the LORD his God give him a lamp in
Jerusalem . . . because David did that which was right in the
eyes of the LORD, and turned not aside from anything that he
commanded him all the days of his life—*save only in the matter
of Uriah the Hittite.*' But the saving clause is absent from the
B text of the LXX. In other words, the Alexandrian translators
ignored the Uriah episode in the third book of Reigns as they had
already done in the second. To them David was a life-long saint.

---

[1] I employ the following symbols. Early portions: ββ (i. e. a section of β) =
2 R. i. 1–xi. 1; γγ = 3 R. ii. 12–xxi. 43. Late portions: βγ (overlapping from β
into γ) = 2 R. xi. 2—3 R. ii. 11; γδ = 3 R. xxii and 4 R. (whole); collectively
these two portions of the 'Decline and Fall' may be cited as βδ.

My second piece of evidence comes from the Chronicler, whose procedure furnished a precedent for our translator. The ' white-washing' had begun already in the third century B.C. The Chronicler closely follows his authority (2 Samuel) up to the point where our translator laid down his pen, 'David tarried at Jerusalem'. Then he ruthlessly curtails, passing over nearly eleven chapters of his source. He was doubtless actuated by the same motive as our translator, though his action was less drastic ; he does not scruple, for instance, to include his hero's sin in numbering the people.

If the evidence so far quoted for a bipartition or expurgated account of David's reign is slight, we have clear and unquestion-able authority for the termination of a volume of the *Reigns* with his death. You will remember that according to the Massoretic division of books David's reign rather oddly encroaches into the first book of Kings, which opens with his old age ; his death is not reached until chap. ii. 11. *The Lucianic recension of the LXX*, however, *unites these sixty-four verses to the preceding book*. This arrangement, by which Book II closes with the death of David, as Book I with the death of Saul, is certainly the more intelligible ; and the evidence from style in the mass of our Greek MSS. corroborates it. The characteristic features of the Asiatic school, which first appear in the Uriah episode, run on into the first sixty-four verses of Book III and then cease. Two lines of evidence thus converge to the same end. The Lucianic recension brings Book II down to the death of David, but its fairly uniform style gives no hint of a change of translators at that point. The uncial MSS. retain the familiar division of books, but their speech— the altered style—bewrays them and confirms the Lucianic tradition. The origin of the other arrangement, which attaches David's old age to the reign of his successor, remains an enigma. I suspect the explanation is to be found in an attempt to make Samuel and Kings into volumes of more equal dimensions.

The Alexandrian translators opened their third book with the accession of Solomon. How far did they carry the narrative of the later Monarchy? I am inclined to place the end of their third volume one chapter earlier than in the printed texts—at the end of the 21st[1] (rather than the 22nd) chapter of 1 Kings (*Baσ. γ*). The later Monarchy did not present any obvious dividing-line, but at this point there did occur a note of time indicating an interval of some duration: 'And they continued

[1] In the Hebrew the 20th ; chaps. xx and xxi being transposed in the Greek.

three years without war between Syria and Israel'. The translator
lays down his pen leaving Israel victorious over Syria. In the
previous verse (xxi. 43) occurs the last well attested instance in
the *Reigns* of the historic present, sure index of the early school.

Internal evidence. Main characteristic of the ' early ' portions. The historic present and its functions.

Turning to the internal evidence on which my theory rests,
I need not dwell on the details.[1] It will suffice to mention the
one outstanding characteristic of the ' early ' school and one or
two prominent features of the later or literalist school.

The main distinctive characteristic of the three ' early ' portions
is the large use of the *historic present*. The following statistics,
taken from the B text, practically hold good for the other
MSS., the Lucianic group excepted. Book a contains 151
examples, $\beta\beta$ 28, $\gamma\gamma$ 48; in all 227 examples, amounting
to not far short of two-thirds of the instances in the whole
of the LXX. Very striking is the contrast when we turn to
the ' late ' portions. Here there are no more than nine examples,
several of which are suspicious :—

In $\beta\gamma$: 2 R. xi. 7 καὶ παραγίνεται (perhaps a doublet of καὶ εἰσῆλθεν which
is unrepresented in M. T.) ; xiv. 27 (two examples of a marriage and birth
unrecorded in M. T.) γίνεται γυνή . . . τίκτει ; in the same context xiv. 30
παραγίνονται (clause not in M. T.); xvii. 17 πορεύονται καὶ ἀναγγέλλουσιν. In
$\gamma\delta$ we have only 4 R. i. 18 a βασιλεύει (clause not in M. T.) and two examples
of ἔστιν for ἦν in vii. 5, 10, which should not strictly be included, since οὐκ
ἔστιν is the invariable rendering of אֵין in this portion. The clauses not
in M.T. are either glosses or possibly relics of a primitive version of
extracts which have been incorporated in the later complete version. It
should be added that in the Lucianic text the historic presents continue
throughout $\beta\delta$ up to the fourteenth chapter of the fourth book, where
they cease.

I must ask for indulgence if I touch briefly on the functions of
this tense, in the Books of Reigns in particular. The Greek use,
I venture to think, has not been generally understood, and our
books are specially enlightening. By substituting the present
for a past tense in narrative the narrator, according to the usual
view, vividly depicts a bygone incident as taking place at the
moment of speech. The tense is commonly described by the
vague epithet ' dramatic '. In our own language the practice has
been wellnigh relegated to the vernacular. We associate a liberal
use of ' Says he ' or ' He comes and says to me ' with persons of

[1] See Appendix I.

the social status of Mrs. Gamp. In the Greek of the classical age
the use was shared by the literary language with the vernacular ;
a growing fastidiousness set in only in the age of the Κοινή.[1]
Its functions may, I think, be more precisely defined than by the
word 'dramatic'. One narrower purpose which it served has
been detected and placed in a separate category. Brugmann
classifies the examples under the two heads 'dramatic' and 'date-
registering'. He traces the date-registering use to the bare
records of births, deaths, &c., in the old chroniclers and genealo-
gists. But the 'dramatic' use seems also capable in most cases
of a closer definition. The present is mainly confined to verbs of
motion (coming, going, sending) ; some writers use it also with
verbs of seeing and saying. But the use with *verba dicendi*
seems always to have been regarded as vulgar. The tense as a rule
is, I believe, 'dramatic' in the sense that *it serves to introduce new
scenes in the drama.* It heralds the arrival of a new character
or a change of locality or marks a turning-point in the march of
events. Even the colloquial λέγει (shunned by the fastidious)
may be brought under the same head. It is the *loquitur* introducing a new speaker. It marks the exact point where *oratio recta*
begins, the past tense being retained even in the verb immediately
preceding ; 'he answer*ed* and saith', ἀποκριθεὶς λέγει in St. Mark,
ὑπολαβὼν λέγει in Job LXX. The main function is thus, I maintain,
to introduce a date, a new scene, a new character, occasionally
a new speaker ; in other words a fresh paragraph in the narrative.

In the 'early' portions of the *Reigns* the tense commonly
serves one of these two purposes : either (1) as date-registering,
or (2) to introduce a new scene like a stage-direction, 'Scene
a battle-field. Enter the Philistines '.

The clearest instance of the date-registering use is the present
βασιλεύει, which, along with θάπτεται, is constant in the recurrent
decease-and-accession formula in third *Reigns*. The formula here
runs 'A slept (ἐκοιμήθη) with his fathers and *is buried* (θάπτεται)
with his fathers, and B his son *comes to the throne* (βασιλεύει) in
his stead '.[2] The Book of Reigns is, as it were, parcelled out into
its component reigns by this device. The present catches the eye
like the underlining of a date. It is noteworthy that here and

---

[1] This will appear from the following statistics collected from the first three
books of each of four leading historians. Herodotus (i–iii) has 206 ; in the
same compass Thucydides has 218, Xenophon 61, Polybius 40.

[2] Note in particular 3 R. xv. 25 Ἱεροβοὰμ βασιλεύει (of the accession) ἐπὶ
Ἰσραὴλ ἐν ἔτει δευτέρῳ τοῦ Ἀσὰ βασ. Ἰούδα, καὶ ἐβασίλευσεν ἐν Ἰσραὴλ ἔτη δύο (of
the subsequent reign).

elsewhere it is the burial, if recorded at all, which stands in the
present, while the death is denoted by the past tense (ἐκοιμήθη);
the interment, not the decease, marks the close of the career.
With this mannerism of the Alexandrian translators we should
contrast the later fourth book, where the formula consistently runs
ἐκοιμήθη-ἐτάφη-ἐβασίλευσεν.[1] In ββ nearly all the examples
fall under the date-registering head: χρίουσιν ii. 4, v. 3 (David's
coronation), ii. 23 (death of Asahel), iv. 7 (death of Mephibosheth),
iv. 12 (death of his murderers), and so on.

A few examples will illustrate the historic present in its other
rôle as 'curtain-raiser' in the drama of 1 Reigns. It occurs first
at i. 19 (of Elkanah and Hannah) καὶ ὀρθρίζουσιν τὸ πρωὶ καὶ
προσκυνοῦσιν . . . καὶ πορεύονται τὴν ὁδὸν αὐτῶν; the scene shifts
from Shiloh to Ramah, and the next words open chapter ii in an
ancient capitulary system.[2] The reason for the next example,
iii. 15 καὶ κοιμᾶται Σαμουήλ, is not so obvious, but we note that
the tense again coincides with an old chapter-opening in the same
MS. Chapter iv opens with a mise en scène depicting the
two armies encamped over against each other with four historic
presents. The main action follows in past tenses, the present
recurring only at the crises: the entry of the ark on the scene
(αἴρουσιν 4), the defeat (πταίει 10), the death of the wife of
Phinehas occasioned by the news (ἀποθνήσκει 20). The presents
of coming and going in chapters v–vii mark the stages in the
itinerary of the ark. In the Goliath episode (xvii) we have
another characteristic mise en scène with eight presents in the first
three verses, beginning Καὶ συνάγουσιν ἀλλόφυλοι . . . and ending
καὶ ἀλλόφυλοι ἵστανται ἐπὶ τοῦ ὄρους ἐνταῦθα καὶ Ἰσραὴλ ἵσταται
ἐπὶ τοῦ ὄρους ἐνταῦθα ('Philistines right, Israelites left', so to
speak). The presents in these proems have to my mind just the
same effect as a stage direction: 'France. Before the gates of
Harfleur. The Governor and some citizens on the walls; the
English forces below. Enter King Henry and his train.'

I can only remark in passing that the presents in St. Mark
(λέγει excluded) are used in a precisely similar way to introduce
new scenes and characters, that they generally coincide with
chapter-openings in the capitulary system in Codex Alexandrinus,
and that St. Luke, in suppressing them, has removed a feature
which to the observant reader serves to divide the older Gospel
into rough paragraphs.[3]

---

[1] For the single exception, 4 R. i. 18 a βασιλεύει, see above.
[2] In cod. M.
[3] Archdeacon Allen adduces the frequent historic presents in St. Mark as an

Characteristics of the ' later' portions.

I turn to the later portions, the ' Decline and Fall'. Besides the avoidance of the historic present, due here probably to literalism—Hebrew had no equivalent—, these portions have their own special characteristics. The common motive underlying most of them is to adhere closely to the Hebrew and to reproduce in the Greek minute distinctions in the original. A few examples will here suffice.[1]

The most arresting is the monstrous use of ἐγώ εἰμι before a finite verb. This solecism marks off the beginning and end of ' the Decline' (βγ); the first instance occurring in Bathsheba's message to David, ἐγώ εἰμι ... ἔχω (2 R. xi. 5), the last in David's death-bed words to Solomon 'I go the way of all the earth', ἐγώ εἰμι πορεύομαι ... (3 R. ii. 2). Then we meet with no more till we reach the fourth book ('the Fall'). This astonishing use is elsewhere practically confined to Aquila and Theodotion.[2] An ellipse of the relative (ἐγώ εἰμι πορεύομαι, e.g. representing ἐγώ εἰμι ὃς πορεύομαι) will not account for all the instances. The barbarism, I have no doubt, is a mechanical expedient for preserving in the Greek the distinction between the two forms of the Hebrew first person pronoun, the longer, and in the translators' day the rarer, ānokī and the shorter ănī. Because anoki sometimes stands for 'I am' the literalist school ordained that it should invariably be rendered ἐγώ εἰμι; the simple ἐγώ being reserved for ani. This rule holds good of all instances except the two last, where the ani of the M. T. has doubtless replaced an earlier anoki.

In vocabulary I can but quote two instances. The same scrupulous preservation of distinctions is seen in the use of κερατίνη for shophar, the ram's horn, while σάλπιγξ is reserved for the haṣoṣerah or straight trumpet of beaten metal. This distinction is again characteristic of the Asiatic school. My second instance I quote because it shows how late, and too often neglected, Κοινή Greek may occasionally throw a reflex light on the classical language. I refer to the peculiar rendering of the Hebrew גְּדוּד (usually meaning 'a band of marauders') by μονόζωνος, a word elsewhere confined in Biblical Greek to two

---

instance of 'Aramaism' (*Studies in Synopt. Problem*, 295, *Expository Times*, xiii. 329); a quite untenable theory. Would he maintain that 1 Samuel lay before the Greek translators in Aramaic?

[1] See Appendix I.

[2] The examples in the B text of Judges and Ruth are doubtless due to Hexaplaric influence.

examples in Theodotion's version of Job. Other LXX books employ λῃστής, λῃστήριον and the like. Μονόζωνος, 'wearing a girdle only' and so 'lightly equipped', is unparalleled outside the Greek Bible; but its poetical equivalent, οἰόζωνος, occurs in a familiar passage in Greek Tragedy, where I venture to think it has been misinterpreted. At a critical moment in the *Oedipus Tyrannus* of Sophocles, Oedipus, as will be remembered, anxiously awaiting the all-important evidence of the herdsman, finds consolation in the thought that rumour spoke of Laius as murdered by robbers (λῃσταί) in the plural. But, he adds,

$$εἰ δ' ἄνδρ' ἕν' οἰόζωνον αὐδήσει, σαφῶς$$
$$τοῦτ' ἐστὶν ἤδη τοὔργον εἰς ἐμὲ ῥέπον.^1$$

'But if he names a single *bandit*, then beyond doubt this guilt is laid at my door.' That surely is the meaning. The contrast is between many λῃσταί and one οἰόζωνος; and in the LXX μονόζωνος is a synonym for λῃστής. With the profoundest respect, therefore, I venture to question whether the late Sir Richard Jebb might not have reconsidered his translation 'if he names one *lonely wayfarer*', had the Biblical use come within his purview.[2] The belt which formed the sole accoutrement of the bandit carried the dirk or παραζώνη, another word peculiar to the 'later' portions of the Reigns.[3]

I must pass over the transliterations in βδ. Transliteration is a hall-mark of Theodotion, and some of the instances here found can only be paralleled from his work.

Is Theodotion or 'Ur-Theodotion' the second translator?

This brief review of some outstanding features of 'the Decline and Fall' might be thought to place the translator's name beyond question. The word μονόζωνος is confined to these portions of the Greek Bible and to Theodotion; Theodotion transliterates the same Hebrew words and in the same way as those transliterated in βδ; and a fairly exhaustive examination of the vocabulary reveals numerous other instances of words peculiar to, or characteristic of, the Ephesian translator.

---

[1] 846 f.

[2] Mr. J. T. Sheppard in his recent edition (Camb. Univ. Press, 1920) follows the lead of Sir Richard.

[3] In 2 R. xviii. 11 in all the texts, *ib.* xxi. 16 in 'Lucian' and Theodotion, in 4 R. iii. 21 in Lucian alone. Usually translated 'girdle'; but note the variants ῥομφαίαν 2 R. xviii. 11 Arm., μάχαιραν *ib.* xxi. 16 Symmachus, and the use of the dimin. παραζωνίδιον for a dagger cited in Liddell and Scott.

The phrase ἐκχεῖν πρόσχωμα, 'to throw up a mound' against a besieged city is restricted to 2 R. xx. 15, 4 R. xix. 32, and Θ Dan. xi. 15; ἐπικαθίζειν as the rendering of רָכַב to βδ (five times) and Θ Is. lviii. 14; τάσσειν (for the commoner στηρίζειν) τὸ πρόσωπον to 4 R. xii. 17 and Θ Dan. xi. 17; καὶ προσέτι renders וְאַף כִּי only in 2 R. xvi. 11 and Θ Job xxxvi. 16 (προσεπιηπάτησεν is an obvious corruption). David, confronted with alternative penalties, exclaims Στενά μοι πάντοθεν (2 R. xxiv. 14); Susannah, surprised by the elders, makes the same exclamation in the version of Θ (v. 22) and the context in both passages mentions the 'luncheon-hour', ὥρα ἀρίστου (2 R. ib. 15; Sus. 13). It is needless to multiply parallels.

Moreover, it is *a priori* probable that recourse would be had to this translator to supplement an imperfect version. This is what happened with the Greek Job. Similarly it was Theodotion's version which supplanted the older paraphrase of Daniel. And it has been conjectured that the two Greek versions of Ezra bear the same relation to each other as the two versions of Daniel; the recurrence of the same transliterations in Esdras B and in Theodotion is, in Mr. Torrey's opinion, conclusive.[1]

That there exists a very close relation between βδ and Theodotion is unquestionable. Yet, on several grounds, I find it impossible to identify our translator outright with the Jew of Ephesus. Were the 'Decline and Fall' the work of Theodotion pure and simple, we should expect to find no evidence from him quoted in Hexaplaric MSS. We do indeed find a paucity of such attestation and are sometimes expressly told that Theodotion agreed with the LXX. There remains, however, a residuum of divergent renderings to be accounted for. Again, there are clear indications that, before the time of Theodotion, Josephus made use of a Greek version of the later Monarchy. Lastly, as Professor Burkitt reminds me,[2] our translation is not made from the Massoretic text, as that of Theodotion practically was.

There remains the alternative that βδ is the work of a 'proto-Theodotion', an anonymous version which Theodotion incorporated nearly entire, introducing some quite minor alterations of his own. I must confess to a prejudice against theories postulating the existence whether of an *Ur-Theodotion* or an *Ur-Marcus*. Yet this explanation accounts for the *data* more satisfactorily than any other. It is, moreover, not unparalleled. In quotations from Daniel the acquaintance shown with Theodotion's renderings, not only by Josephus but even by New Testament writers, has

[1] *Apparatus for Textual Criticism of Chronicles-Ezra-Neh.* (Chicago, 1908.)

[2] He calls attention to a clear instance in 2 R. xvii. 3 where the M. T. has dropped several words and the Greek has preserved the longer and better reading.

forced critics to the conclusion that, unless Theodotion's date was pre-Apostolic, he must have freely borrowed from an earlier lost version. There is no improbability in such a lost original. Many persons took in hand to improve upon the LXX, and Origen discovered fragments of three other versions besides those of known parentage.

Our translator appears to have been a *pioneer* of the literal school and a *predecessor* of Aquila. He has advanced to the stage of equating ἐγώ εἰμι with *ānokī*, but has not taken Aquila's further step of representing אֶת (the mark of the accusative) by σύν. Some of Aquila's renderings read like simplifications of those of βδ. Thus he replaces the rare and perhaps provincial μονόζωνος by the classical εὔζωνος. The same relation holds good, I think, between two words (πάροδος, παροδίτης) which I will take as my final test-words.

For illustration of LXX Greek we normally turn to the Egyptian papyri. Here we must look to Asia and the inscriptions. The inscriptions enable us to localize within a narrow area one item in the vocabulary of our translator and to claim it as a characteristic of Asiatic Greek. The word, moreover, is one in which our translator parts company with Theodotion. Our object is to get behind Theodotion to his forerunner and to determine his provenance.

In Nathan's parable we read that 'there came a *traveller* unto the rich man' (2 R. xii. 4). In his Greek dress this traveller has something to tell us of his travels. The Greek word in all our MSS. except the Lucianic group is πάροδος. Lucian and Theodotion write the classical ὁδοιπόρος; Aquila has παροδίτης, which also has ancient authority. A feminine πάροδος we know; πάροδος, masculine for 'a traveller', is a solecism of extreme rarity. Symmachus, probably an Asiatic, has it once (Jer. xiv. 8). In the LXX so-called, we meet it again only in Ez. xvi. 15, 25. But that chapter is probably not Alexandrian work; it is just such another passage, like the Uriah episode, as the original translators would readily omit, containing a scathing indictment of Jerusalem under the figure of a harlot making advances to every passer-by (παντὶ παρόδῳ).

Outside the Greek Bible ὁ πάροδος is confined to sepulchral inscriptions on or connected with the western sea-board of the Levant.[1] We find throughout Greece, the Aegean islands, and the Levant a practice of appending to a sepulchral inscription

---

[1] I have searched the papyri in vain for a parallel.

a greeting from the dead to the way-farer. The word 'way-farer' takes two forms. Sometimes in verse, occasionally with variants like χαίρειν τοῖς παράγουσιν (or τοῖς παρερχομένοις), the normal phrase is either χαῖρε παροδεῖτα or χαῖρε πάροδε. I have counted upwards of forty examples with παροδ(ε)ίτης, seven only with πάροδος.[1] Παροδίτης is invariable on the mainland of Greece, throughout both the Peloponnese (Laconia, Messenia, Arcadia) and Thessaly; Boeotia shows a variant form παροδώτης. Proceeding north we find it in the island of Thasos, near Adrianople, and at Perinthus on the north coast of the Propontis. Only when we cross to the west coast of Asia and the adjacent islands do we meet the alternative πάροδε; first at Mytilene in Lesbos, then at Smyrna, then inland at Laodiceia, which has both forms, and again in the island of Cos, which shows similar fluctuation. Westwards of Cos and well out on the route to Greece, the island of Amorgos reverts to the Hellenic παροδ(ε)ίτης (over twenty examples), with a single exception; πάροδε occurs once in the township of Aegiale, which, since the third century B.C., was under Milesian rule; the conquerors imported the Asiatic idiom. This exhausts the instances of πάροδος, with one highly significant exception, in the far west. It is on a monument erected in Italy to a boy of nine years old by his father, who describes himself as Λαοδικεὺς τῆς Ἀσίας; he has carried overseas the provincialism of his home in the Lycus valley. Laodiceia is the only point inland to which, to our knowledge, this form penetrated; did it travel thither from the coast by the high-road from Ephesus or by river from Miletus? Neighbouring Hierapolis shows παροδ(ε)ίτης only, and eastwards in central Phrygia, that form, so far as our evidence goes, is universal.[2] Πάροδος is thus confined to the area embracing Lesbos, Smyrna, Aegiale, and probably its mother-city, Miletus, Cos, and Laodiceia — a district having for its focus Ephesus, the home of Theodotion. Ephesus itself yields no evidence; the sleepers of Ephesus have no blessing, only curses, for the intruder. Yet Theodotion himself consistently writes

[1] See Map at end of volume.

[2] The examples of πάροδος noted are as follows: MYTILENE, Berlin Corpus of *Ins. Graecae*, vol. xii, pt. ii, no. 410; SMYRNA, Boeckh, *C. I. G.*, vol. ii, 3273; LAODICEIA, *ib.*, vol. iii, 6512 (inscr. in Rome) and Ramsay, *Cities and Bishoprics of Phrygia*, vol. i, p. 78, App. i. 13; AEGIALE (in AMORGOS), Berlin *I. G.*, vol. xii, 445; Cos, R. Herzog, *Coische Forschungen* (1899), nos. 133 and 163. The examples of παροδ(ε)ίτης have been collected from the Berlin Corpus, Ramsay, *op. cit.*, and (for Perinthus) *Jahreshefte des Österreichischen Arch. Institutes in Wien*, Bd. i. (1898).

ὁδοιπόρος. In our Greek Bible (if I may so put it) Nathan's
traveller is a bourgeois from Asia; Theodotion, himself an Asiatic
of no mean city, presents him as an Athenian gentleman. In plain
language, to me this instance is conclusive proof that our translator
was a western Asiatic, but not Theodotion. Theodotion merely
appropriated his neighbour's version. To this anonymous *Asiaticus*
we owe the completion of the unfinished work of Alexandria.

The Company of Prophetical Translators

From the 'Reigns' or 'Early Prophets' I turn to the 'Later
Prophets' (from Isaiah to the Twelve), the translation of which
was doubtless the first to be taken in hand after the Pentateuch.
Here there were, I think, two stages: first a rendering of select
passages appointed as lessons for the festivals and special sabbaths;
secondly a complete version. The earlier stage will be illustrated
in my next lecture. To-day I am concerned with the complete
version, which must soon have superseded the lectionary extracts,
and in particular with Jeremiah. The Greek here gives us two
clues as to the procedure and personnel of the translators. It
indicates (1) a practice of dividing the longer books into two
approximately equal parts, (2) that the work was the outcome
of co-operation of a *company* of translators, analogous to the
pioneering company which gave us the Greek Pentateuch.

The work of this second company embraced, if I am not
mistaken, Jeremiah, Ezekiel, and the Twelve. The Isaiah
translator stands apart. The treatment of divine names often
affords a ready criterion, and in the phrase YHWH SABAOTH
the Isaiah translator, in common with the first book of Reigns,
leaves the second word in its Hebrew form (Κύριος σαβαώθ), while
the 'group', in so far as they use the phrase, translate by
'Almighty' (Κύριος Παντοκράτωρ). Though the question is
important, I must not stop to consider the reason for this isolation
of Isaiah and whether the translation succeeded or, as I incline
to think, preceded the group.

The links which unite the group are two. On the one hand,
the Greek Jeremiah and Ezekiel curiously resemble each other
in that a change of style, in other words of translators, occurs in
the middle of either book. In Jeremiah the break comes in
chap. xxix of the Greek text, in Ezekiel at or about the beginning
of chap. xxviii. The books differ in one respect. In Jeremiah the

distinctive marks of the second style continue to the end.[1] In Ezekiel the second style, beginning in the middle, persists for a dozen chapters (xxviii–xxxix), when the first style is resumed. For convenience I shall refer to the two pairs of translators as Jer. α and β, Ez. α and β. Broadly speaking, Jer. α translated the first half, Jer. β the second half of his book. Ez. α besides the first half undertook also the last quarter, including the hardest parts of his prophet; the share of Ez. β being restricted to the third quarter. Now, when we find two contiguous prophecies bisected in this way (for it is important to note that the central break is purely mechanical, not governed by subject-matter), we begin to suspect co-operation of a company, who for greater expedition have agreed upon a division of labour. The impression is strengthened by the second link, that of style. Jer. α and Ez. α have many features in common; but it is the δωδεκαπρόφητον which is here of primary importance. I have failed to discover any similar mechanical break in the Book of the Twelve; but in style and vocabulary the Greek Minor Prophets as a whole bear so close a resemblance to Ez. α as to suggest that these large portions of the LXX may have been rendered by a single individual, some leading spirit in the little company. Jer. β and Ez. β stand apart; having their own idiosyncrasies besides points of contact with the other members. The translation of these portions seems to have been left to subordinates, the lesser lights of the company.

THE TRANSLATORS OF JEREMIAH

The Greek Jeremiah has probably provoked more inquiry than any other Septuagint book, owing to its exceptionally wide divergence from the Hebrew. The main difference between the two texts consists in the dislocation and rearrangement of one section, the group of prophecies against Foreign Nations. The divergence affects the position assigned to the group as a whole and the order of the individual prophecies. We have a similar series of prophecies against Foreign Nations in Isaiah and Ezekiel, where they occupy a central position. In the Greek Jeremiah the Oracles similarly stand in the centre of the book, immediately after a sentence common to both texts (xxv. 13) which seems to lead up to them. In the Hebrew, however, they are relegated to a final, or penultimate, position, being followed

---

[1] Excluding the Historical Appendix (chap. lii).

only by the Historical Appendix (chap. lii) which has no claim
to prophetic authorship. Again, in the Greek the separate
prophecies are unsystematically arranged.[1] In the Hebrew they
stand in a fairly orderly geographical sequence, proceeding
eastwards from Egypt to Babylon.

This varying position of the Oracles has long since led critics,
from Eichhorn and Bertholdt in the eighteenth century to Duhm
in the twentieth, to conjecture that the Book of Jeremiah is
a compilation of two or more smaller volumes. The unfortunate
prophet has suffered Isaiah's traditional fate in being sawn
asunder, with the added barbarity that the operation has been
performed at different places. According to the latest theory,
that of Duhm (the most brilliant of German exponents of the
Prophets), there were two books: (1) chaps. i–xxv of the Hebrew,
which he entitles 'The Book of the words of Jeremiah'; (2) the
remainder (xxvi–lii), comprising, in his opinion, large extracts
from a lost Book of Baruch, a biography of the prophet, which
once had an independent existence as a *historical* book. These
extracts have been collected by an editor and expanded into
a second book of Jeremiah by the addition of a little book of
consolation (xxx–xxxi Heb.), the Oracles and the Historical
Appendix.

That our Book of Jeremiah is a compilation from smaller
collections is indisputable.[2] But such theories as I have
mentioned rest on no secure basis; the Oracles against the
Nations, which seem to hold the key to the riddle of the two
texts, are attached by one critic to the first volume, by another
to the second. The advocates of a two-volume Jeremiah have
strangely overlooked the evidence afforded by the LXX. To
that evidence I will confine myself, without venturing on
precarious theories as to ultimate origins. In the Greek we do
find clear and unmistakable signs of bisection, but the phenomena do not support any theory of two self-contained volumes.
The division is purely mechanical, and yet appears to go back
behind the Greek to the original Hebrew.

It will suffice to quote a single instance of the variety of
styles in the Greek Jeremiah, a cogent criterion on which

[1] Except that the three world-empires (Elam, Egypt, Babylon) precede the
smaller nations bordering on Palestine.

[2] We need not go beyond the opening verses (i. 1–3) for witness to its
gradual growth. The story of Baruch, after the burning of the first roll,
rewriting the whole and adding thereto 'many like words' (xxxvi. 32) points
in the same direction.

implicit reliance might be placed even if it stood alone. The Alexandrians were not rigidly consistent in their renderings. We have to allow for some natural variety; and in looking for proofs of a plurality of translators, it is sometimes difficult to find test-phrases that are absolutely convincing. Here we are fortunate enough to discover a diversity of rendering in the commonest of Hebrew phrases running right through the book. The alternative renderings are consistently adhered to on either side of a central line. The phrase is כֹּה אָמַר יְהֹוָה, 'Thus saith (or "said") the LORD'. This is rendered (1) by τάδε λέγει Κύριος upwards of sixty times in the first half (down to xxix. 8); (2) by οὕτως εἶπεν Κύριος some seventy times in the latter half.[1] The last occurrence of τάδε λέγει opens the prophecy against Edom (xxix. 8): the prophecy upon Ammon opens with οὕτως εἶπεν (xxx. 1). Between these two occurs in our oldest uncials, B and ℵ, a unique instance of the mixture τάδε εἶπεν.[2] Seldom, I think, can the higher critics of the Hebrew Pentateuch adduce so convincing a proof of the limits of the component documents J and E—or, I might add, of the intervention of the compiler JE, though I should not lay stress on the unique τάδε εἶπεν— as is here afforded of the limits of the respective work of a pair of translators.

A glance at the Concordance will show numerous other instances of discrepancy between the two parts, on which I need not dwell. Certain words are represented only up to the 28th (or 29th) chapters; others make their first appearance at that point.

Hebrew had another formula for introducing the words of the Deity, נְאֻם יְהוָה 'Oracle of Jahweh'. a renders נְאֻם by λέγει, not distinguishing it from אָמַר; β ordinarily by φησίν. Among nouns 'time' in a is καιρός, in β χρόνος; 'joy' in a is χαρά, in β χαρμοσύνη. 'I will light a fire' in a is ἀνάψω πῦρ, in β καύσω πῦρ; 'to receive (education)' in a δέξασθαι, in β λαβεῖν (παιδείαν); the respective portions have ἰᾶσθαι ἰατρεύειν for 'heal', κατασκηνοῦν καταλύειν for 'dwell' or 'tabernacle', παροργίζειν (παρα)πικραίνειν for 'provoke'. And so on.

Then we have instances where β adopts an a word but gives it a nuance of his own or coins another word from it; the two translators have co-operated. Thus while a employs the adjective ἄβατος, 'trackless' or 'desert', β uses the neut. ἄβατον as an abstract noun 'desolation' and coins ἀβατοῦν, 'to render desolate'. Similarly β seems responsible for coining the substantive ἰταμία from the adj. ἰταμός in a.[3]

[1] Down to li. 34. The phrase is absent from the Appendix.

[2] xxix. 13. Of the converse mixture οὕτως λέγει I have noted four examples in the B text, two in either part, viz. xiv. 10, xxiii. 16; xli. 4, xlii. 13.

[3] For further details see Appendix II.

The general results which emerge are as follows. The line of demarcation falls somewhere in the latter part of chap. xxix. (Gr. text). A mixture of styles occurs at the juncture; the actual point of transition cannot be fixed to a verse. The line cuts the group of Oracles in two, four (or five) nations standing on the one side, the remainder on the other. The bisection goes back as far as the textual history can be traced. The double vocabulary is prior to the earliest version made from the LXX, the Old Latin; Tyconius preserves the distinction between τάδε and οὕτως, though disregarding the distinction of tenses, writing 'Haec dicit', 'Sic dicit' respectively in the two portions. It antedates the Asiatic school; for Aquila, consistent as he normally is, sometimes follows the LXX variety of translation.[1] We cannot definitely say that the double vocabulary is older than New Testament times merely because the first half is practically unused; but in the Epistle to the Hebrews (viii. 8 ff.) we have a long citation containing the characteristic marks of Jer. β. Behind New Testament times external evidence fails us; but I think we may confidently assert that the distinction in style between the two parts has stood in the Greek ever since a complete version of Jeremiah existed. One further remark. The line of demarcation cuts across and *presupposes* the LXX arrangement of chapters with the Oracles in the centre of the book. The translators are not, it seems, responsible for the dislocation.[2] For, whoever effected the drastic and arbitrary transposition of these chapters clearly regarded the Oracles as a unit. Were the translators responsible, the point selected for the second translator to take over the work is likely to have fallen on one side or the other of the transposed block. In fact the translators have ignored the unity of this section and drawn their line right through the middle of it.

That translator β was the weaker scholar of the two appears from some curious examples of what may be called 'imitation Hebrew' or the employment of words or phrases of which the only link with the Hebrew is a resemblance in sound, while they entirely fail to reproduce the sense. They recall the schoolboy's 'howler'. Some of these may be due to later corruption; to Hellenization, i.e. an endeavour to extract an intelligible Greek meaning out of an original transliteration.

---

[1] Thus 'time' (עֵת) in *a* is καιρός, in β χρόνος; Aquila ordinarily employs καιρός but once (xxxvii. 7) follows β in writing χρόνος.

[2] Cf. p. 36 below for a further proof of this.

Others, though pure guesses, are so curiously felicitous in their context that I cannot but think they go back to the original translator. Such errors might arise through mishearing, if, as seems probable, the method employed was dictation and two workers co-operated, one dictating the Hebrew and occasionally assisting with the Greek, the other confining himself to translation. A Hebrew word dictated by the one might be mistaken by the other for a Greek rendering.

The following examples may be quoted :—(1) הֵידָד (the word for the rhythmical cry of the vintage-gatherers as they trode the grapes in the wine-vats, onomatopoeically rendered *ià ià* by the 'Syrian' translator, with local knowledge) is represented by αἰδε Jer. xxxi. 33, οἰδε xxxii. 16. Probably a scribal 'improvement' upon an original αἰδέδ or ἠδάδ (cf. Aq.), as the pron. ὅδε occurs nowhere else in Jer. β. Jer. α, through confusion of ר and ד, renders οἱ καταβαίνοντες xxviii. 14. (2) 'The men of Kir-heres' become ἄνδρας κειράδας (xxxi. 31, cf. 36), meaning apparently 'the shorn men', which is in keeping with the context (37) 'Every head shall be shorn and every beard clipped' in token of mourning. (3) xxxviii. 9 αὐλίζων (ἐπὶ διώρυγας ὑδάτων) 'providing a lodging' answers to Heb. אוֹלִיכֵם 'I will bring them'. Gr. probably due to mishearing of dictated Heb. The theme is the common one in Deutero-Isaiah, &c., of Israel's happy home-coming with God for their leader and nature conspiring to ease their journey. (4) xxxviii. 21 Στῆσον σεαυτήν, Σειών, ποίησον τιμωρίαν, Heb. 'Set thee up waymarks (צִיֻּנִים), make thee guide-posts' (תַּמְרוּרִים) on the road to Palestine. Probably due to the translator; reprisals on Israel's foes are a standing feature in the Zionistic programme. But corruption has affected the following clause; correct ὤμους to οἴμους (with Streane). (5) xli. 5 ἕως ᾅδου (κόψονταί σε) for Heb. הוֹי אָדוֹן 'saying) Ah! Lord'. Jer. α writes correctly οὐδὲ μὴ κλαύσονται αὐτόν Ὄιμοι κύριε xxii. 18. Cf. xxix. 6 where הוֹי is represented, if at all, by the definite article ἡ (ἡ μάχαιρα). (6) Cf. also two examples where the Gr. καί corresponds to Heb. כִּי 'because', xlii. 16, xliv. 16. (5) and (6) may be explained by dictation.

It remains to mention some of the rarer instances of *agreement* between the translators. In the forefront stands the rendering of the Divine Name יהוה צבאות by Κύριος Παντοκράτωρ which runs right through Jeremiah and the Minor Prophets. With this may be connected another title found in both parts of the Greek Jeremiah, and, except for its model, nowhere else. In the description of his call (i. 6) the prophet tries to evade his onerous commission on the ground of youth and inexperience. The verse runs in the Greek καὶ εἶπα Ὁ ὢν δέσποτα Κύριε, ἰδοὺ οὐκ ἐπίσταμαι λαλεῖν, ὅτι νεώτερος ἐγώ εἰμι. For ὁ ὢν δέσποτα Κύριε, 'O thou (self-)existent sovereign Lord', the M. T. has אֲהָהּ אֲדֹנָי יהוה 'Ah Lord God'. Clearly the translator in place of the interjection אֲהָהּ read אֶהְיֶה and had in mind the call of Moses and the Divine Name by which God then revealed Himself אֶהְיֶה אֲשֶׁר אֶהְיֶה (Ex. iii. 14), with the LXX rendering Ἐγώ εἰμι ὁ ὤν ... ὁ ὤν ἀπέσταλκέν με. The reminiscence was the more natural seeing that the lawgiver sought to evade the responsibilities of office on the same grounds as the prophet. Now this interpretation of אֲהָהּ recurs in both parts of Jeremiah (xiv. 13; xxxix. 17); whereas elsewhere in the LXX we find οἴμμοι or μηδαμῶς (Ez.), ἆ ἆ or δέομαι.

Incidentally we may note a parallel case of a description of a call to office being modelled on that of a predecessor. In St. Paul's speech before Agrippa (Acts xxvi. 15–18) the Apostle (or his biographer) reports the terms of his commission in language reminiscent of the call of no less than three prophets, Ezekiel, Jeremiah, and the Lord's servant in deutero-Isaiah (cf. Ez. ii. 1; Jer. i. 8; Is. xlii. 7 ff.). And that the biographer is not wholly accountable appears from the Apostle's own allusion to his conversion in Gal. i. 15, where the words ὁ ἀφορίσας με ἐκ κοιλίας μητρός μου καὶ καλέσας are based on the call of the Lord's servant (Is. xlix. 1).

The translators were at one in their treatment of Divine titles; they were united also in their reverent attitude to the deity. Jeremiah with bold Hebrew anthropomorphism represents JHWH as 'rising early' and sending His prophets or performing similar actions. Our pair of translators hit upon the same expedient to avoid what they regarded as an irreverent phrase; they write 'in the morning' (ὄρθρου). In the only passage where the literal ὀρθρίζων is allowed to stand (xxv. 3) the subject of the verb is not JHWH but the prophet.

Further instances of the translators' agreement are mainly confined to the use of some rare Greek words. In the recurrent phrase 'in the cities of Judah and in the streets of Jerusalem' the Greek in both parts for 'in the streets' has ἔξωθεν (Ἰερουσαλήμ), twice in Pt. I (xi. 6, xxviii. 4), more often in Pt. II (xl. 10, li. 6, 9, 17, 21; cf. Baruch ii. 23). This is one among many indications that the translators' exemplar, in both parts, employed abbreviations. Terminations were often omitted, and בְּחוּצוֹת was read as בָּחִיץ. The confusion is peculiar to Jeremiah. (Similarly, in both parts יהוה was often expressed by a single Yôdh; and the abbreviation was confused with the suffix of the first pers. pronoun, e.g. θυμόν μου vi. 11, θυμοῦ μου xxxii. 23, Heb. 'the wrath of JHWH'.) Rare Greek words peculiar to these two translators are: ἄμφοδον a block or 'island' of buildings, Heb. אַרְמוֹן 'palace' (xvii. 27; xxx. 16); καταράκτης for 'the stocks' as instrument of torture, an unparalleled use (xx. 2 f.; xxxvi. 26); χαυῶνες, Hellenization of כַּוָּנִים 'cakes' (vii. 18; li. 19); συμψᾶν, 'sweep away' (xxii. 19; xxix. 21, xxxi. 33). The phrase 'the corner-clipt', of a foreign mode of cutting the hair, is similarly paraphrased in both parts: περικείρεσθαι (τὰ) κατὰ πρόσωπον (ix. 26; xxxii. 9, cf. xxx. 10).

The general result of the investigation is that we find a cleavage with a distinct vocabulary on either side of chap. xxix together with a few striking instances of agreement. I can only account for the phenomena by imperfect collaboration of two workers, the second of whom only partially followed the lead of the first. The translator of the first half was the superior. Clearly it was he who in the opening chapter made the happy discovery of the analogy between the call of the lawgiver and that of the prophet, whose book had been entrusted to his charge ; his partner merely followed suit. The scholarship of the latter, if he is responsible for some flagrant 'howlers', was weak, and his inclusion in the company is surprising. It would seem that in weightier matters, the treatment of the Divine titles and one expression needing reverent handling, as also for a few rare words, he sought help from his colleague and a mutual agreement was reached. Generally, however, rigid uniformity was not aimed at, and the inconsistency in the rendering of the common formula 'Thus saith' escaped detection. How easily this might happen I know from personal experience. I did not discover this, the most cogent proof of the double vocabulary, until the last.

Our own Authorized Version of the New Testament owes some of its inconsistencies to much the same cause, a lack of adequate supervision and communication between two isolated companies sitting at Oxford and at Westminster.[1]

One question remains. Were the translators the first to break the book into two in the middle of the Oracles, or had they warrant for so doing in their Hebrew exemplar ? I think they had such warrant. The Hebrew text yields two pieces of evidence (1) in the titles to the Oracles, (2) in the colophons appended to two of them.

(1) The titles fall into two categories, long and short. The long titles all ascribe the particular prophecy to Jeremiah and add information as to date or occasion of delivery. The short titles, with one exception, consist merely of the name of the nation preceded by the preposition ל, 'concerning Edom', &c. The important fact is that with the Hebrew order of nations long and short titles are intermixed; the arrangement seems haphazard and *only becomes explicable if the Oracles are read in their Greek order.* Read in that order, we have six long titles,

<hr />

[1] See the Revisers' Preface.

beginning 'The word of JHWH that came to Jeremiah the
prophet concerning Elam in the beginning of the reign of
Zedekiah, king of Judah', and so on, followed by five shorter
titles, 'Of Edom', &c., with only one approach to a fuller statement. Two results follow. (i) When the titles were inserted,
the chapters were arranged as in the LXX. They are a witness
to the priority of that arrangement. (ii) They afford *Hebrew*
evidence for a break or interruption in the middle of the Oracles.
The longer titles cease at about the end of Part I. The line of
demarcation, by this test, falls between Philistia and Edom,
a line practically identical with that drawn by the change in
the Greek style.[1] I conclude that our translators in their
division of labour did not act on their own caprice ; they merely
followed a division which they found already in their Hebrew
exemplar. The Hebrew editor who amplified the titles apparently had only Part I before him and did not carry his work
further.

(2) The Hebrew contains two colophons which are not in the
Greek. Their similarity of form suggests that they come from
one hand. In xlviii. 47 (Heb.) we read 'Thus far is the judgement of Moab'; in li. 64 (Heb.) 'Thus far are the words of
Jeremiah' (at the close of the Babylon Oracle). The second
colophon is explained by the Hebrew arrangement, in which
Babylon is not only the last of the nations, but rounds off the
whole book apart from the Historical Appendix (lii), which the
colophon-writer definitely pronounces to be no part of the
prophet's work. The first colophon is explained by the Greek
arrangement. In the Hebrew Moab stands in an intermediate
position, where no remark is called for. But in the Greek it is
the last of the nations, and the note calls attention to the fact.
I infer that the Hebrew editor was familiar with both arrangements of the Oracles and probably wrote these colophons at the
time when the rearrangement took place.[2] While indicating
that in the Revisers' opinion the Nations and the whole book
should close with Babylon, he thought fit to preserve an indication
of the older tradition by writing 'Thus far is the judgement
of Moab'.

The Greek translators, I conclude, utilized for their own

---

[1] Edom is on the border-line and cannot with certainty be assigned to either
Part.

[2] Probably in the first century A. D., when Babylon had become a pseudonym
for Rome.

purposes an already existing division of Jeremiah into two volumes. The second volume was no self-contained unit. It had no formal opening and merely carried on the series of Oracles with which Vol. I broke off. The volumes have ragged edges. Moreover, and this point I would emphasize, Jeremiah does not stand alone. The practice of a mechanical bisection of books, at least the longer books, finds parallels in other parts of the LXX. For the explanation we must look, I believe, to what the Germans call *Buchwesen*, to something in the *format* and make-up of the Hebrew rolls, in modern language to the bookbinding or possibly the booksellers' department.

The Translators of Ezekiel

In conclusion, I can but glance at the phenomena presented by the Greek version of Ezekiel. The analogy to Jeremiah is curiously close. Again we have a mechanical bipartition of the book for translation purposes. The transition again occurs in the middle of a group of Oracles against Foreign Nations. I place it within the long Oracle against Tyre, at the point where the prophet turns from the city to denounce its prince. The name of the city, which in chaps. xxvi–xxvii is the Hebraic Σόρ, from xxviii. 2 onwards takes the ordinary Hellenized form of Τύρος. But again, as in Jeremiah, a certain mixture of styles at the juncture leaves the exact point of transition doubtful; it might be placed a little earlier.

That the central dividing-line is drawn mechanically is shown by the translators' neglect of a more obvious division which lay ready to hand. The book comprises two main themes, Destruction and Reconstruction, and falls accordingly into two parts of twenty-four chapters each, the second part opening with the Oracles against the Nations, which form the prelude to the prophecies of Restoration. This distinction of subject-matter was well-known to the Rabbis, who observed that Ezekiel opens with desolation and ends with consolation, and fancifully traced in this the reason for its being placed, as early tradition placed it, after Jeremiah, which is all desolation, and before Isaiah, which is all consolation.[1] Nevertheless, the translators went out of their way to find a still more equal division with the measuring-line.

Beside these resemblances, the translation has its differences

---

[1] T. B. *Baba Bathra*, 14 b (translated in Ryle, *Canon of O. T.*, p. 274).

from the Greek Jeremiah. In Ezekiel, in addition to the central break, we find a second break at xl. i, coinciding with an obvious change in subject-matter. The three divisions are thus (1) chaps. i–xxvii which I call Ez. a^i, (2) chaps. xxviii–xxxix Ez. β, and (3) chaps. xl–xlviii Ez. a^{ii}. But, though we have this threefold division, there are, as in Jeremiah, two main translators and two only. The final portion, with the picture of the ideal Temple and the future disposition of regenerate Israel, notwithstanding the widely different topics with which it deals, presents so many similarities of language to the first portion that the two are undoubtedly the work of a single translator (Ez. a). The leader, beside his first half, has appropriated also the last quarter. His reappearance at the close supports the belief that the pair were contemporaries co-operating on a common task. There is no inherent reason for the omission of the dozen chapters comprizing Ez. β. A roughly equal initial division of labour, with the resumption of the task by the leader at a point where it seemed beyond the capacity of a subordinate, adequately accounts for the facts.

In another particular the versions of Jeremiah and Ezekiel differ. We find in the latter one outstanding patch, the Greek of which cannot be ascribed to either of the pair. Within the province of Ez. β there falls a short section of fifteen verses (Ez. xxxvi. 24–38, with the promise of 'the new heart') in another style; the translators have here, I believe, incorporated an older version made for lectionary use in the synagogue.[1] As already suggested (p. 26), the unedifying chapter xvi was perhaps omitted by the Alexandrian company, and the Greek in our texts is a later supplement.

Detailed proofs of this threefold division appear elsewhere.[2] Here I can but mention two instances. The Appendix (chaps. xl–end) with its distinct topics lacks the Hebrew phrases characteristic of the rest of the book. We can therefore point to no one ubiquitous test-phrase comparable to 'Thus saith YHWH' in Jeremiah. Instead, we may take a phrase which in the first two portions may be considered the *leitmotif* of the prophet. 'They shall know that I am JHWH' in a^i is normally ἐπιγνώσονται διότι ἐγὼ Κύριος, in β γνώσονται ὅτι ἐγώ

---

[1] See Appendix III (4).

[2] See Appendix III, for further details, and Appendix IV for further proofs of the prevalence of the 'half-book' practice in Jewish antiquity, of which we have found examples in Jeremiah and Ezekiel.

εἰμι Κύριος; here there are three minor differences. In another constant phrase 'Prophesy and say' (lit. 'Thou shalt say') α[i], adhering to the Hebrew, writes προφήτευσον καὶ ἐρεῖς; β has two imperatives προφήτευσον καὶ εἰπόν.

In contrast to his subordinate colleague β, who does not reappear in the LXX, Ez. α was a master who played a prominent part in the translation of the Nebiim. I will end with a brief reference to these wider activities of his. Not only did he appropriate three-quarters of Ezekiel, but he is also apparently responsible for the version of the bulk, if not the whole, of the Minor Prophets. But, if I am not mistaken, his energies did not stop even here. On a fresh reading the conviction has grown upon me that it was he who gave us, in part at least, the third book of Reigns, the Greek narrative of Solomon and the divided Monarchy. It seems probable that the Alexandrian expurgated version of the Reigns was likewise the work of a company. Our translator was a member of that other company as well, unless indeed the companies were one and the undertaking on a still larger scale. The evidence is clearest in the sections relating to the two Temples, Solomon's and Ezekiel's, where there is a remarkable agreement in the architectural terms, alike in the Greek renderings and in the transliterations. But there are other parallels scattered sporadically over the two books. Most remarkable of all is a rendering due, it seems, to mispronunciation—to an error in dictation. Through confusion of gutturals, נ and ע, גְּלוּלִים 'idols' is constantly rendered in Ez. α by ἐπιτηδεύματα (= עֲלִילוֹת); this error recurs only in 3 R. xv. 12. The text of 3 Reigns has reached us in a disordered state. I do not, of course, maintain that our translator is responsible for the whole text as it stands in codex B. The parallels with Ezekiel α come in clusters, from which we may roughly estimate the extent of his handiwork. These groups include some of the obviously early portions, the precious fragment from the Book of Jashar and the alternative story of the disruption, peculiar to the B text. These same paragraphs also contain striking parallels to the δωδεκαπρόφητον.[1]

[1] See Appendix III (3).

LECTURE II

THE SEPTUAGINT AND JEWISH WORSHIP

(1) The Feast of Pentecost

I HAVE taken as the theme of my second and third Lectures certain Jewish festivals and fasts and the portions of Scripture used, or designed for use, on those occasions in the services of Temple or synagogue. My aim is to show that these passages cannot be fully understood without regard to their employment in public worship. The liturgical use is, I venture to think, a factor in exegesis which has been unduly neglected. The subject deserves fuller treatment than I can give it by some expert in Hebrew and Rabbinical lore. Such constructive work as has been done on these lines we owe mainly to Jewish scholars. Our English commentators have too often disregarded Jewish tradition concerning lessons or Psalms proper to special occasions, as having no bearing on interpretation. The traditions, it is true, were not committed to writing before (at earliest) the second century of our era, but there is good reason for thinking that they or some of them were inherited orally from earlier generations. The liturgical use, I maintain, goes well back into pre-Christian times, before the text was finally fixed, and has in various ways influenced and moulded the form in which the text has come down to us. In the selection of the passages recited or chanted *analogy* played an important part. Analogy with the first lesson determined the choice of the second ; and this process of assimilation was carried further, and the several portions of Scripture employed on the same occasion tended to react on each other and to be affected by the dominant notes of the ritual. Jewish worship was homogeneous ; the service was no medley of incongruous hymns and prayers. Lessons and Psalms had an affinity to each other and to the ritual. We need then to restore to their original setting, and to study the mutual connexions between, passages which were associated in ancient worship.

The field of inquiry is limited, but deserves working out. It is practically limited to the prophetical lessons and Psalms for the principal Feasts and Fasts and a few special sabbaths. I do not maintain that the text of the Pentateuch was affected. It had wellnigh reached its final form when the custom of public reading was introduced, and was probably read in its entirety when the Greek translation appeared. On the other hand, the text of the Prophetical books had not, it seems, been stereotyped when, about 200 B.C., they were received into the Canon and short extracts began to be read on the festivals. At that very time the Alexandrians were engaged in producing a Greek version. The final compilation of the Psalter followed later. It is here, I think, that this line of inquiry may prove specially fruitful. It has been increasingly recognized that such internal evidence as the Psalms afford is insufficient to determine with certainty the date and occasion of writing. The occasions on which some of them were employed in public worship we know; and we may obtain light on details if we approach their study from this point of view before attacking the problem of remoter origins. Liturgical glosses may be looked for especially at the beginning and end of a Psalm or adjacent to the liturgical 'Selahs'.

The Septuagint, which doubtless owed its existence to the lectionary needs of a Greek-speaking community, furnishes important; but not the only, evidence in the investigation. To the LXX evidence I shall devote special attention, while touching on other illustrative material. I was first attracted to this line of research by the accidental discovery of an obscured rubric embedded in a Greek version of an old Pentecost lesson. Later I had the good fortune to find that the Greek rendering of an obscure passage in the Psalm for the Feast of Tabernacles was elucidated by the companion lesson. My lecture to-day will be devoted to those and other passages employed at these two festivals.

I must begin with some preliminary remarks on the evolution (1) of the Jewish festivals, (2) of the lectionary system.

(1) The inquiry is pushed back to festival origins by the recurrence of certain dominant notes in the cultus, which are reflected in the lessons. One is driven to ask, How did these *motifs* arise? In a fascinating chapter of his *Prolegomena* Wellhausen long ago reconstructed the history of the evolution of the Jewish festivals from a primitive agricultural stage to what may be called the priestly and historical stage.[1] On the settlement in Canaan the Israelites took over, along with the land, the agri-

[1] *Prolegomena to History of Israel*, Engl. trans. 1885, chap. iii, 'The sacred feasts'.

cultural feasts of the conquered people, with the profound difference that JHWH replaced Baal as the object of worship. The
feasts were purely agricultural without historical associations.
The spring Feast of Unleavened Bread (*maṣṣoth*) marked the beginning, the summer Feast of Harvest (*Ḳaṣir*; afterwards Weeks,
Shabuoth, or Pentecost) the end, of the corn-harvest, while the
autumn Feast of Ingathering (*Asiph*) or Booths (*Succoth*) celebrated
the vintage and olive harvest, the winding up of the agricultural
operations of the year. Associated with the spring festival was
another which came to be called Passover; probably the oldest of
all, originating in a pastoral period before the settlement, when
the offering consisted of the firstling of the flock.

That was the primitive stage. In the final stage, represented
by the Priestly Code, much of this original character is lost. The
feasts, no longer movable and dependent on weather conditions,
now have fixed dates assigned to them, and—the main innovation
—now primarily commemorate crises in the national history.
The spring festival recalls the liberation from Egypt, the slaying
of the firstling of the flock the slaying of the first-born, the unleavened bread the haste of the departure. Pentecost—though
this identification came later—celebrates the law-giving on Mount
Sinai. Lastly, the booths of the vintage-gatherers stand for the
hut-dwellings of the Israelites during their forty years' wanderings. Egypt, Sinai, Wilderness: the feasts now mark the stages
on the route to Canaan.

On the pagan origin of the festivals I would make one comment. Wellhausen speaks of the primitive 'solar' festivals. The
context shows that by 'solar' he means merely 'seasonal', 'those
which follow the seasons of the year'.[1] I would venture to
suggest that some of the popular ceremonies, those portions of
the cultus which are most tenacious of pagan relics, contain indications of 'solar' connexions in the strict sense; indications,
I mean, of an association of the feasts with the cardinal points in
the sun's apparent movements in the heavens, the equinoxes and
solstices, the *Tekuphoth* as the Hebrews called them. The
evidence is clearest in the feast of most recent institution. To
the three great festivals was added in post-exilic days a fourth,
that of the Dedication, instituted in 164 B. C. by Judas Maccabaeus
to celebrate the rededication of the Temple after its desecration
by Antiochus Epiphanes. Falling on the 25th Kislev (approximately our December) and popularly known as the 'Feast of

[1] *Prolegomena*, p. 83.

Lights ', illumination figured prominently in the cultus, and the fables which gathered round it [1] relate to a miraculous kindling of fire. The popular custom of the kindling of lights in the home, increasing on each evening of the feast from one to eight,[2] undoubtedly symbolized the growing light of the year. Judas, it seems, reconsecrated a pagan 'Shortest day' carnival, just as old pagan festivals of the solstices were rechristened as the birthdays of John the Baptist and of our Lord. The Dedication feast was modelled on that of Tabernacles.[3] Tabernacles, Philo tells us,[4] fell at the autumnal equinox, and the most popular ceremony was a great illumination of the Women's Court of the Temple *ending with an express disclaimer of sun-worship*. Passover approximately synchronized with the vernal equinox. Pentecost alone occupies an abnormal position, being fixed, when precise dates were introduced, a month before midsummer. Whether it supplanted an older midsummer festival it would be rash to speculate.[5]

The hierarchy subordinated but could never suppress these pagan associations, and relics of the nature religion survived in practices known to us only from the Talmud.

(2) For the evolution of the lectionary system our main ancient authority is the tractate *Megillah* in the Babylonian Talmud. In modern times we owe most to some classical articles by Dr. Büchler in the *Jewish Quarterly Review*.[6]

We know from the scenes at Nazareth [7] and Pisidian Antioch [8] that lessons were read on the sabbath from both Law and Prophets in New Testament times. The Torah readings were already a long-established and widespread institution. Moses from generations of old had his preachers in every city, being read in the synagogues every sabbath.[9] The custom began, it seems, with short lessons on the Festivals and on four extraordi-

---

[1] Narrated in 2 Maccabees.

[2] According to the school of Shammai the number decreased from eight to one; Oesterley-Box, *Religion and Worship of Syn.*[2], 404.

[3] The author of 2 Macc. (i. 9) calls it ' the feast of tabernacles of the month Chislev '.

[4] *De spec. Leg.* ii. (*de Septen.*) 204 (24).

[5] The curious omission of Pentecost from his festival-scheme by Ezekiel, who deplores the Tamuz- and sun-worship of his time (viii. 14 ff.), is perhaps significant.

[6] Vols. v. (1893) 420 ff. and vi. (1894) 1 ff.

[7] Luke iv. 16 ff.   [8] Acts xiii. 15.   [9] *ib.* xv. 21.

nary sabbaths. These primitive festival lessons, we may confidently assert, were all taken from a single chapter, Lev. xxiii, containing a catalogue of feasts with instructions as to ritual. The Mishna names lessons from this chapter for three festivals [1] and the same rule doubtless once applied to all. The practice, in Dr. Büchler's opinion, had a controversial origin. It was the Palestinian method of meeting the attacks of Samaritans or Sadducees, who showed their animosity by unorthodox explanations of the por- tions of the Pentateuch relating to the festivals.[2] Controversy waxed warmest over an arithmetical problem. The Feast of Pente- cost or Weeks was peculiar in that it took its names not from its nature, but from the interval separating it from the previous feast or more precisely from the ceremony of waving the first sheaf of the harvest. The Leviticus passage (xxiii. 15 f.), from which the original lesson must have been taken, ran 'And ye shall count unto you *from the morrow of the sabbath*, from the day that ye brought the sheaf of the wave-offering . . . fifty days'. But 'the morrow of the sabbath', from which the reckoning started, was ambiguous. The orthodox view was that 'the sabbath' meant the first day of the Feast of Unleavened Bread, no matter what the day of the week; the Sadducees identified it with the ordinary sabbath falling within the festal week. The Alexandrian translators mark their orthodoxy by rendering 'on the morrow of the first day' ($\tau\hat{\eta}$ ἐπαύριον τῆς πρώτης).[3] It is not surprising that this contentious lesson was abandoned. Our oldest authority, in fact, names as the lesson not the Leviticus passage, but the parallel one in Deut. xvi. 9 ff., in which the time- statement, though indefinite, lacked this particular ambiguity : 'Seven weeks shalt thou number unto thee : from the time thou beginnest to put the sickle to the standing corn shalt thou begin to number seven weeks.' Dr. Büchler is convinced that this lesson supplanted an older one from Lev. xxiii; the LXX, as will appear, supplies the requisite missing evidence.

These festival lessons from Leviticus were the first stage. The next was probably the introduction of weekly sabbath readings

[1] Passover, New Year's Day, Tabernacles.

[2] 'The people had to be taught . . . how to meet their attack; this could not be better achieved, or in a simpler manner, than by reading and explain- ing the disputed passages in the Pentateuch on the Festivals themselves which had been made the subject of controversy,' *J. Q. R.* v. 424.

[3] Lev. xxiii. 11, cf. 16. In the intervening occurrence of the phrase (*v.* 15) they are content with a literal version, having already shown what meaning they attach to 'sabbath'.

according to a triennial cycle. The Pentateuch was divided into some 150 sections and was read through once in three years. On this system, which was in vogue in New Testament times and was generally superseded by an annual cycle about A. D. 200, I need not dwell.

The *Haphtarah* or prophetical lesson began with the reading on the festivals of a few verses in illustration of the Torah lesson; its length was gradually extended. It is at this stage that the LXX, now coming into existence, gains importance. The earliest lessons seem to have been drawn from the Minor Prophets, Ezekiel and Jeremiah.

The *Haphtaroth* for certain feasts and fasts present common features which may throw light on the origin of the second lesson. (1) The selected passage in several instances occupies a position at the end of a book. The last chapters of Habakkuk, Zechariah, Hosea, Isaiah were all so employed. These final chapters are probably foreign to the books to which they are attached. (2) Several lessons are *poems*, which again are suspected of being interpolations in their prose context. We have the Psalm of Habakkuk, taken, as we are told, from the Precentor's collection, and the Song of Hannah; while the nucleus of the lessons for the Day of Atonement (from Jonah) and for the Feast of Tabernacles (from 1 Kings viii) was probably in the one case the song of Jonah in the whale's belly, in the other the Song of Solomon, drawn, as the LXX tells us, from the Book of Jashar. I infer that before the formal reception of the prophetical books into the Canon, the custom had already grown up of chanting a canticle, or reading some edifying passage, as a sequel to the Leviticus lesson, and that this passage became the nucleus of the *Haphtarah*. 'It is probable', wrote the present Dean of Westminster, 'that the adoption of a lesson from " the Prophets " corresponded with the period of their admission into the Canon', which he dates about 200 B.C.[1] If, as I venture to suggest, the way had already been paved for a second lesson, there would be a tendency to retain the familiar words and to regularize their use by engrafting them into the new prophetical collection. This would account for the poetical form, the incongruity, and the final position of these festival *Haphtaroth*. A final position would incidentally assist the reader to find the place.

Another device for this purpose, to enable the reader to find the second lesson—no easy task in a roll lacking chapters and

[1] *Canon of Old Testament*, 116.

verses—was the catchword system.[1]   If we may judge by later
practice, each section of the Law was given a label, consisting of
the first or the first distinctive word or words or indicating the
general contents.   This catchword was then written in the margin
over against the corresponding lesson in the prophetical roll.
Thus if the first lesson was labelled 'Jethro', the reader of the
second would open his roll until his eye lit upon the marginal
note 'Jethro'.

For the *Psalter* the LXX titles already indicate the Psalms
appointed for daily use.   For the festival Psalms, doubtless the
first to be used in worship, our fullest extant authority is the
tractate *Sopherim*, which, though dated as late as A.D. 800, preserves traditions of a far earlier age.[2]

FEAST OF PENTECOST

I pass to Pentecost, the Feast of Wheat-Harvest and the Law-
giving.   Our oldest authority, the *Megillah*, names alternative
lessons: from the Law Deut. xvi. 9 ('Seven weeks') or Ex.
xix (the story of Sinai), from the Prophets 'Habakkuk' or 'the
Chariot' (Ez. i); adding that now that the festival lasts two days
all four lessons are used.   This statement dates from the age of
the Tannaim, from the first or second century of our era, and
looks back to a remoter period of a one-day feast.   When was
the second day added?   The author of the *Book of Jubilees*, writing about 100 B.C. (Charles), in describing the institution of
Pentecost, lays such emphasis on its being confined to 'one day in
the year' (this is repeated thrice) as to raise a suspicion that he
is combating an innovation of adding a second.[3]   The lessons are
therefore certainly as old as A.D. 100, possibly as early as 100 B.C.

The proper Psalm according to the tractate *Sopherim* is xxix
Afferte Domino, according to Rabbinical authorities lxviii *Exurgat
Deus*.

I am not directly concerned with the lessons from the Torah.
The Sinai lesson was probably that for the second year in the
Triennial Cycle; it is thought that the accident of its being read
at this season originated the tradition that the Law was given at
Pentecost.   My observations will be confined to the *Haphtarah*
from Habakkuk and the two special Psalms.

---

[1] The first lesson, being drawn either from a single chapter or, later, from
a continuous series, would present no difficulty.

[2] *Masechet Soferim*, ed. J. Müller (1878), p. 22.

[3] Chap. vi. 17-22 (trans. Charles, 1902).

The common theme which runs through all four passages from Prophets and Psalter is a theophany in thunder-storm, a triumphal march or ride of the deity across desert, sea or heavens amid a general convulsion of nature. In Habakkuk: 'Thou didst march through the land in indignation', 'Thou didst ride upon thy horses, thy chariots of salvation', 'Thou didst tread the sea with thine horses'. Ezekiel pictures the vehicle of the deity (the *Merkabah*) and the living creatures supporting it. In Ψ. xxix, under the image of the seven-fold voice of JHWH, we see the thunder-storm sweeping across Palestine from Lebanon to Kadesh. In Ψ. lxviii: 'When thou marchedst through the desert', 'Cast up a highway for him that rideth through the deserts', 'The chariots of God are twenty thousand', 'Make melody to him that rideth upon the heavens'. With these passages should be linked one other, on which two of them are dependent, the blessing of Moses in Deut. xxxiii ('The LORD came from Sinai'); and, though authority is lacking, I suspect that it too was employed at Pentecost, as a canticle.

Whatever the origin of this primitive Saga of the divine chariot-drive or theophany in thunder-storm,[1] it is natural to infer that it was the parallels with the terrors of Sinai which lent the passages their appropriateness to Pentecost in the view of those who selected them. On the other hand, the association of Pentecost and the law-giving lacks early authority, being strangely ignored by the Old Testament, Philo,[2] and Josephus; and I cannot but suspect that the 'chariot-drive' with the attendant convulsion of nature has behind it some older pagan meaning, such as the great journey from one end of heaven to the other of the midsummer sun and the violent thunder-storms characteristic of that season.

THE PSALM OF HABAKKUK

I come now to the 'Prayer' or Psalm of Habakkuk (Hab. iii), the lyric ode appended to the prophecy, which, in the words of the late Dr. Driver, 'for sublimity of poetic conception and splendour of diction, ranks with the finest which Hebrew poetry has produced'.[3] Its beauty is unfortunately marred by some grave obscurities.

---

[1] 'Gewitter-Theophanie': Gunkel, *Schöpfung und Chaos*, 106.

[2] Philo, *De spec. leg.* ii. 22 (188 ff.) transfers the law-giving to the autumn Feast of Trumpets. The trumpet denotes (1) that of Sinai (Ex. xix. 16); (2) the θεήλατος πόλεμος ὅταν ἡ φύσις ἐν ἑαυτῇ στασιάσῃ.

[3] *Introd. to Lit. of O. T.⁴*, 317.

Broadly speaking, the nineteen verses fall into three portions:
(1) the opening prayer, (2) the theophany (*vv.* 3–15), (3) a beautiful passage about the harvest, which has proved or promises to
prove a failure, beginning 'For though the fig tree shall not
blossom And no fruit be in the vines' and ending 'Yet will I
rejoice in JHWH, I will joy in the God of my salvation'.[1]   The
theophany is doubtless the oldest portion, which has been expanded for liturgical purposes.   The passage about the harvest
has been penned, it seems, for a harvest festival.   The words
look on beyond the wheat-harvest to the autumn ingathering of
vine and olive, and, if a bad year is anticipated, this may reflect
the Pentecostal custom of reciting the curses upon disobedience.[2]
The theophany, with reminiscences of Sinai, is equally apposite.
Pentecost commemorated both wheat-harvest and law-giving; it
is this double commemoration alone which binds the two main
portions of the poem into a coherent whole.

   This Pentecostal use is strangely overlooked by the commentators, and I approached the study of the poem quite unaware of
it.   Its attraction for me was the peculiarity that two independent Greek versions have survived.   On the one hand is what
I will call the normal text, represented by the bulk of the MSS.
and in the printed editions; on the other a version which appears
in four MSS. only, two in Italy and two at Oxford.[3]   The normal
version is in the style of the Greek Minor Prophets as a whole;
it is part and parcel of the larger work of the company of which
I spoke in my last lecture.   The peculiar, or 'Oxford', version is
to all appearance older, betraying the marks of high antiquity.
It is, I believe, a precious relic from the first stage in the Greek
version of the Prophets—the rendering of extracts appointed for
lectionary use on the festivals.   In describing the versions as
independent, I should exclude the first two verses, where the
texts are practically identical.   This, however, is due to confla-
tion; these verses are made up of 'doublets'; an early editor has
amalgamated two rival renderings of the exordium.

   [1] The Blessing of Moses (Deut. xxxiii) supplies the model for the beginning
(*v.* 3) and end (*v.* 19 'He will make me to walk upon mine high places') of the
two main portions.
   [2] Büchler in *J. Q. R.* v. 440 quoting T.B. *Meg.* 31 b. Cf. Lev. xxvi. 16, 20
'Ye shall sow your seed in vain ... your land shall not yield her increase,
neither shall the trees of the land yield their fruit'.
   [3] V (= 23) at Venice; 86 (Rome, Barberini); 62 and 147 (Oxford). The
aberrant text is printed in E. Klostermann's *Analecta zur Septuaginta*, 50 ff.,
and in Field's *Hexapla*.

Obscured rubrics. The whole Psalm deserves careful study, but I am primarily concerned with a few words only, in which I discovered, as I believe, some obscured rubrics. The use as a Jewish canticle is patent; the musical rubrics appear on the surface. The lectionary rubrics are there too, but concealed. The poem seems to be scored with the marks of ancient liturgical use.

(1) I turn first to the colophon or docket at the close : in the Hebrew 'For (or Belonging to the collection of) the Chief Musician on my stringed instruments'.[1] The rubric, it must be remembered, would follow the poem immediately without break. The official 'company' of translators had, therefore, some excuse for failing to recognize its nature. They incorporated it into the Psalm, and, interpreting the participle of נָצַח ('Director' or 'Choir-master') in its later sense of 'conquer', produced the rather ridiculous ending 'He sets me upon the high places *to conquer in his song*' (τοῦ νικῆσαι ἐν τῇ ᾠδῇ αὐτοῦ).

The translator of the rival version has something quite different, viz. the two words ταχίσας κατεπαύσατο, 'He made haste and stopped' or, more probably, 'caused to cease', 'gave rest'. Peace after storm, after the terrors of the theophany, that was the meaning he extracted from the Hebrew before him. The phrase unquestionably represents a Hebrew original; it is not, as has been suggested,[2] a scribe's idle comment on the brevity of the Book of Habakkuk! Doubtless this translator also erred through misinterpreting a rubric. What rubric stood in his text? For it is impossible to extract his rendering from the note about the Chief Musician. Now κατεπαύσατο is the natural equivalent for הִשְׁבִּית 'caused to cease', the hiphil of שָׁבַת 'rest'; and this at once suggests misreading of הַשַּׁבָּת 'the sabbath'; the two would be indistinguishable in an unvocalized text. Again, the Hebrew equivalent for ταχίσας, 'quickly', is מְהֵרָה, and מָהֳרָה with the slightest of alterations becomes מָחֳרַת 'morrow of'. I concluded that the translator found in his Hebrew מָחֳרַת הַשַּׁבָּת 'morrow of the sabbath'. This conjecture, I must repeat, was reached in ignorance alike of the Pentecostal associations of the Psalm and of the phrase 'morrow of the sabbath' and the storms which had raged over it; I had no preconceived ideas and failed at first to grasp the sense of the restored rubric. I am not taking credit to myself; I was lamentably ignorant. But my ignorance had its

---

[1] לַמְנַצֵּחַ בִּנְגִינוֹתָי.

[2] By the late Dr. Sinker, *Ps. of Hab.* (Cambridge, 1890).

D

compensation in strongly confirming my belief in the conjecture
on which I had blindly stumbled, as its meaning dawned upon
me. ' Morrow of the sabbath'; in the light of the lectionary
history we at once recognize the phrase thrice repeated in connexion with Pentecost in Lev. xxiii (vv. 11, 15 f.) and found
nowhere else in the Old Testament. The note is a lectionary
'catchword', indicating by its position ' Here endeth the second
lesson for Pentecost', while its substance tells us what was the
first lesson. No catchword would so readily recall the Leviticus
lesson as this notoriously controversial phrase. The restoration
supplies the missing evidence that Pentecost, like other festivals,
drew its oldest Torah lesson from Lev. xxiii. It suggests, moreover, that the aberrant Greek version was made from an ancient
synagogue roll, designed for lectionary use.

(2) This discovery had to be followed up, and I was lured into
the fascinating study of the origins of Jewish worship. The clue
may have led me too far in the quest for catchwords. I found
none outside this Psalm, but I did discover, as I thought, two
similar notes in the body of it. The natural place for them is
at the point where the text is interrupted by the musical note
Selah. Dr. Briggs remarks on the tendency in the Psalter to
insert glosses before the Selahs.[1]

Our Psalm contains three Selahs. The first of these (in v. 3) is
represented in the Oxford version by *two* Greek words, $\mu\epsilon\tau\alpha\beta o\lambda\grave{\eta}$
$\delta\iota\alpha\psi\acute{a}\lambda\mu\alpha\tau os$. Judging by Ψ. ix. 17 where the Greek $\mathring{\phi}\delta\grave{\eta}$ $\delta\iota\alpha$-
$\psi\acute{a}\lambda\mu\alpha\tau os$ represents two Hebrew words, I infer that our trans-
lator found another word in his original before Selah. Can it be
accidental that $\mu\epsilon\tau\alpha\beta o\lambda\acute{\eta}$, which occurs only twice again in the
translated books of the LXX, in one passage (Is. xxx. 32) corre-
sponds, rather strangely, to תְּנוּפָה ('shaking') and that תְּנוּפָה is
the technical term for the ' wave-offering' mentioned in the same
opening verse of the Leviticus lesson (xxiii. 15): 'And ye shall
count unto you from the *morrow of the sabbath* from the day that
ye brought the sheaf of the *wave-offering* . . .'? I conjecture,
with diffidence, that this is another reference to the first lesson.
A different catchword is used, and its position shows that the
Habakkuk lesson was once limited to two verses. A verse or
two, we know, was the usual extent of the oldest *Haphtaroth*.

(3) Again, just before the second Selah in v. 9 we find this
time in the Hebrew (as well as in both Greek versions) some incongruous words interrupting the grand description of the theo-

[1] Psalms (*Internat. Crit. Comm.*), vol. I. lxxxv ff.

phany. A row of three substantives without preposition, suffix, adjective, or other adjunct, they stand in the M. T. SHEBUOTH—MATTOTH—OMER, 'Oaths—Rods (or Tribes)—Word'; and their interpretation has taxed the ingenuity of the translators. Our Revisers, with a stretch of imagination, render ' *The* oaths *to the* tribes *were a sure* word'. The normal Greek text, as acutely restored by Nestle,[1] had 'Seven sceptres saith the LORD'. The Oxford version, most ingeniously of all, produces a rendering in keeping with the preceding line (R.V. 'Thy bow was made quite bare') viz. 'Thou hast glutted the shafts of its (or "his") quiver'. But 'shafts' are not the same as 'rods' and the rendering is suspicious. I have no doubt whatever that the first word SHEBUOTH ('Oaths') should be pointed SHABUOTH ('Weeks'), and little doubt that the LXX 'seven' should be prefixed to it and we should read 'SEVEN WEEKS'.[2] 'SEVEN WEEKS' is the name given in the Mishna to the Deuteronomy lesson which superseded the lesson from Leviticus. The note is presumably Palestinian and may be expanded thus: '*Here*, at *v.* 9, endeth the second lesson for Pentecost. Do not, like our brethren of Alexandria, read either less or more. And the first lesson is "Seven weeks" (Deut. xvi); it is not *our* custom to read from Leviticus.'

In the other nouns 'Rods' and 'Word', with a variant for the second in the Oxford version which I read as 'Jethro', I saw a row of catchwords to the Torah lessons for each year of the triennial cycle. JETHRO meant the Sinai lesson (Ex. xviii-xx, the modern name for it); RODS the lesson about Aaron's rod that budded (Num. xvii. 16 Heb.); WORD or PROMISE [3] the lesson from Genesis xii, the first promise to Abraham. But the lessons for the triennial cycle are only approximately known, and I admit that these identifications are questionable.

The attendants of the Deity (v. 5). Turning from rubrics to the poem itself, I can but touch on a single verse, in which Greek mythology has left its mark on one (if not both) of the Greek translations. Indeed, the original Hebrew of this old Jewish song seems to contain a mythological and semi-pagan element.[4] The grim retinue of the Deity is thus described (*v.* 5): 'Before his

---

[1] Reading ἑπτὰ (for ἐπὶ τὰ) σκῆπτρα, λέγει Κύριος.

[2] שְׁבָעָה שָׁבֻעֹת.

[3] As suggested to me by Professor Burney; cf. Ψ. lxxvii. 9 (Heb.).

[4] The Deity of the theophany is *El*, as distinct from JHWH of the opening prayer, and in *v.* 4 is unmistakably compared to the sun. I suspect that, in the oldest form of the poem, *El was* the sun-god Shemesh; the same transformation has, according to Dr. Briggs, taken place in Ψ. xix.

face goeth *Deber* and *Resheph* goeth forth at his feet.' *Deber* is
Pestilence personified. *Resheph* is commonly interpreted either
as 'fire-bolt' or as 'Fever'; but the word will call for further
remark. The picture recalls a similar procession in the Babylonian account of the Deluge, where Ramman the storm-god has
for one of his attendants the female counterpart of *Deber*,
Dibbarra, goddess of Pestilence.[1] But it is the curious Greek
translations with which I am concerned.

First the Oxford version. ' Before his face shall go πτῶσις.' (this,
as elsewhere in the LXX must mean 'Plague') 'and at his feet
shall follow—τὰ μέγιστα τῶν πετεινῶν, the largest of the birds '!
A grotesque picture, raising the difficult question of the meaning
which the Jews attached to the word *Resheph*. Besides this
passage it occurs five times in the Old Testament and once in the
Hebrew of Ecclesiasticus. Our R. V. consistently renders by
'flame' or 'fire-bolt'; but there is a widespread ancient tendency, not confined to the LXX, to explain it in terms of ornitho-
logy, as meaning either a bird or a wing. In the Song of Moses
(Deut. xxxii. 24) we read of rebellious Jeshurun ' devoured by
Resheph ', R. V. ' with burning heat' (margin 'burning coals') ;
but the LXX, along with Aquila and Onkelos, has ' devoured by
birds' (βρώσει ὀρνέων). In Job v. 7 'the sparks' (the *B'ne
Resheph*, Resheph's brood) which ' fly upward' become in the
Greek young vultures or eagles: νεοσσοὶ δὲ γυπὸς (v. l. ἀετῶν) τὰ
ὑψηλὰ πέτονται. In Cant. viii. 6 the fiery flashes of love appear
as wings (περίπτερα). In the beautiful picture in Sir. xliii. 17 of
falling snow 'settling and loosely lying', the parallel clause suggests that the Hebrew writer himself refers to winged creatures :
' Like *Resheph* (Gr. ὡς πετεινὰ καθιπτάμενα) he sprinkleth his
snow | And as the lighting of the locust is the descent thereof.' [2]

I know of no etymological justification for these renderings,
and can only suppose that the explanation is to be sought in the
attributes of the *god Resheph*. *Resheph* was a Phoenician solar
deity who figures in North Semitic Inscriptions in the company
of *Shamash*, the sun-god, and *Rekabel*, the rider- or chariot-god ;
in bilingual Cypriote inscriptions the name is translated Apollo.[3]

---

[1] ' Ramman caused his thunder to resound; | Nabu and Sharru marched at
the foot | . . . Dibbarra lets loose her mischievous forces' (tr. Jastrow, *Religion
of Bab. and Ass.* 500).

[2] The Greek Psalter alone interprets otherwise, rendering in lxxviii. 48 (Heb.)
by τῷ πυρί, in lxxvi. 4 by τὰ κράτη (? read κέρατα); in both passages Symmachus
writes οἰωνοί.

[3] Prof. G. A. Cooke, *North Semitic Inscriptions*, 55 ff. ; cf. Kraeling, *Aram
and Israel* (New York, 1918), 122.

In Palestine he gave his name to the coast-town of Arsūf, the ancient Apollonia (Apollo-town); and M. Clermont'Ganneau in a suggestive paper has shown reason for identifying him, with metathesis of consonants, with the Greek Perseus.[1] The myth of Perseus and Andromeda is linked to the neighbourhood of Arsūf, the town of *Resheph*.

To return to Habakkuk, what did this old translator mean by τὰ μέγιστα τῶν πετεινῶν, which he refrains from naming? (There was evidently felt to be something uncanny about *Resheph*; Jerome in this passage identifies him with the devil.) I am tempted to find the answer in the wonderful 'flying creatures' called 'phoenixes and chalkadri', in 'size nine hundred measures' which 'attend the chariot of the sun', and are described in an Alexandrian work dated early in the first century A.D.[2] It is, however, perhaps unnecessary to go outside the Bible for the explanation. The 'eagles' of the Job translator *may* give the clue and the birds in Habakkuk be identified with the living creatures of Ezekiel's vision, of which it is said that 'they four had also the face of an eagle'. If so, this is an instance of one Pentecost lesson being interpreted in the light of the other.

The treatment of *Deber* and *Resheph* in the normal Greek text is even more remarkable. Here we find an unmistakable, if veiled, allusion to Greek mythology. In this version the Deity has but one attendant, Λόγος, 'the Word'. *Dĕber*, 'Pestilence', has been read as *Dābār*, 'Word', a fitting forerunner to the Divine law-giver. *Resheph* becomes a mere attribute of Λόγος. The Hebrew (רֶשֶׁף לְרַגְלָיו) is taken to mean not 'Resheph at his feet', that is behind El, but 'Resheph to (or "on") his feet', that is the feet of Λόγος. The oldest form of this peculiar rendering is preserved in cod. A and runs:

πρὸ προσώπου αὐτοῦ πορεύσεται Λόγος καὶ ἐξελεύσεται,
ἐν πεδίλοις οἱ πόδες αὐτοῦ.

---

[1] Also—*mirabile dictu*—with St. George, the patron saint of England; Ganneau; *Horus et St. Georges* (Paris, 1877), cf. G. A. Smith, *Hist. Geog. of Holy Land*, 129 n. 1, 163 f. That *Resheph* should represent both Perseus and Apollo is not unreasonable; on coins of Tarsus hero and god are brought into the closest relation; Ramsay, *Cities of St. Paul*, 152; Imhoof-Blumer in *Journ. of Hell. Studies*, xviii. (1898) 171 ff. The hero must stand for some attribute of the sun-god, possibly the wings of the solar disk.

[2] *Book of the Secrets of Enoch* (ed. Charles), cap. xii; cf. the description of the phoenix which accompanies the sun and screens the earth from its rays in the Greek Apocalypse of Baruch (ed. M. R. James in *Texts and Studies*, vol. V., 1897, Apoc. of Baruch, § 6).

'His feet are in sandals' is the translator's paraphrase of '*Resheph* on his feet'! We know of the fleet-foot Λόγος from the Psalmist: '*He sendeth out his commandment upon earth; his word runneth very swiftly.*'[1] But whence come the sandals? Remembering the Greek connotations of *Resheph*, we cannot doubt that *winged* sandals are intended, and we at once recall the πτηνὰ πέδιλα that carried Perseus over sea and land; and M. Ganneau has already taught us that Resheph and Perseus are one. The Λόγος shod in the sandals of Perseus! No wonder the Septuagint was suspect. Only to an Alexandrian could have occurred so daring and impious an association of things pagan and divine. I scrupled to impute the blasphemy even to an Alexandrian until I found confirmation for it. Hippolytus, in his *Refutation of all heresies*, tells us (iv. 49) of certain heretics who gave an allegorical explanation of the constellations as described in the *Phenomena* of Aratus. They identified Cepheus with Adam, Cassiopeia with Eve, Andromeda with the soul of Adam and Eve, Perseus with the Λόγος, the winged offspring of Zeus (τὸν Περσέα Λόγον, πτερωτὸν Διὸς ἔγγονον), and so on.[2] But the bare hint of such pagan ideas in Scripture was intolerable. Fortunately an easy remedy was to hand. By the omission of one letter ἐν πεδίλοις became ἐν πεδίοις (so Irenaeus, *in campis*); this was again altered to εἰς πεδία (so the B text), and this in the Lucianic recension was finally 'improved' into εἰς παιδείαν! The sandals are decently buried. The Word now goes forth 'for instruction'; the commandment is sent out upon earth. The adaptation to the Feast of the Law-giving is complete.

In the next verse (6) the Oxford text, with the slightest of emendations, comes to our aid. The R. V. runs:

> He stood, and measured the earth;
> He beheld, and drove asunder the nations.

'Measured', which editors wish to alter to 'shook', should stand. The error lies in the last verb. 'Drove asunder' is the rendering of an otherwise unattested hiphil of נָתַר 'spring up", lit. 'made to start up'. The true text is concealed in the aberrant Greek text

$$\kappa\alpha\tau\alpha\nu o\acute{\eta}\sigma\alpha\varsigma\ \grave{\epsilon}\xi\acute{\eta}\kappa\alpha\sigma\epsilon\nu\ ^3\ \tau\grave{\alpha}\ \check{\epsilon}\theta\nu\eta.$$

---

[1] Ψ. cxlvii. 15.

[2] The rationalistic interpretation of Perseus which follows is interesting. Περσεὺς δὲ ἐστὶν ὁ ὑπόπτερος ἄξων, ὁ περαίνων ἑκατέρους τοὺς πόλους διὰ μέσης τῆς γῆς καὶ στρέφων τὸν κόσμον.

[3] So cod. 62; ἐξείκασεν V, 86, 147.

Ἐξήκασεν, 'made like', is unmeaning; but the alteration of one letter at once gives us ἐξήτασεν, 'inspected', 'explored', shows that the Hebrew verb is not נָתַר but תּוּר 'spy out' and produces a well-balanced parallelism :—

> He stood, and measured (or 'surveyed') the earth;
> He beheld, and explored the nations.

The Psalmist again yields a parallel, though the Hebrew verb is different (Ψ. xi. 4) :

> JHWH is in his holy temple,[1]
> JHWH, his throne is in heaven ;
> His eyes behold,[2] his eyelids try (LXX ἐξετάζει), the children of men.

The advance of the Deity is stayed. Motionless overhead in the zenith, with all-embracing glance He surveys the earth and its inhabitants from one horizon to the other. It is the hush before the storm.

In verse 11 the same verb (עָמַד 'stood ') is used of sun and moon as in v. 6 of the Deity. I will venture only two remarks on this corrupt passage. (1) The text in none of its forms speaks of the withdrawal or obscuration of the luminaries, which commentators read into it, but either of a standing still or of an elevation. (2) The fine simile (in v. 10) of the tossing sea 'lifting up its hands on high' (רוֹם יָדֵיהוּ נָשָׂא) must be sacrificed. The parallelism of clauses does not call for another clause answering to 'The deep uttered his voice', but does demand a predicate for שֶׁמֶשׁ, which in the Massoretic text stands without copula before יָרֵחַ; 'Sun, moon stood still in her lofty abode '. The predicate for the sun must be sought in the previous line; the Greek texts favour this construction. The most curious of these is the Complutensian τὸ ὕψος τῆς φαντασίας αὐτοῦ (מַרְאֵהוּ for יָדֵיהוּ) ὑψώθη ὁ ἥλιος, which I take to mean 'The sun was raised to the (full) height of its appearance ', in other words stood at its highest station in the heavens, was at the solstice. I do not suggest that this clumsy phrase represents the original Hebrew, which was probably something like אוֹר נָשָׂא שֶׁמֶשׁ 'the sun lifted up its light' (רוֹם being a gloss); merely that the translator perhaps saw an allusion to the solstice. It is curious that the sole occurrence in the LXX of the technical term for the solstices is in the chapter so closely linked with Pentecost (Deut. xxxiii. 14 ἡλίου τροπῶν).

PSALM XXIX

I pass to the Pentecost Psalms. The LXX here does not materially assist us and my remarks will be brief.

Psalm xxix, *Afferte Domino*, was sung on several festivals.

---

[1] An echo of Hab. ii. 20 which opens the modern Pentecost lesson.
[2] + εἰς τὴν οἰκουμένην cod. U.

Our main authority, *Sopherim* (xviii. 3), assigns it to Pentecost.[1]
The body of it depicts, under the figure of the seven-fold voice of
JHWH, the course of a thunder-storm from Lebanon to Kadesh.
It opens and closes with a picture of the celestial worshippers.[2]
It is this quasi-liturgical setting which is of interest.

In the opening verse the LXX has an additional line, familiarized
by its presence in our English Prayer Book :—

$$'Ενέγκατε\ τῷ\ κυρίῳ,\ υἱοὶ\ θεοῦ,$$
$$[ἐνέγκατε\ τῷ\ κυρίῳ\ υἱοὺς\ κριῶν]$$
$$ἐνέγκατε\ τῷ\ κυρίῳ\ δόξαν\ καὶ\ τιμήν.$$

The second line is obviously a duplicate of the first, due to
misreading of בְּנֵי אֵלִים (the anthropomorphism of which was
distasteful to the translator) as בְּנֵי אֵילִים. But the reading
was facilitated by the fact that rams were among the offerings
prescribed for each of the festivals on which the Psalm was used.
Ritual has affected text.

The conclusion runs :—

And in his palace all are saying 'Glory'.

This recalls Hab. ii. 20 (the opening verse of the modern Pentecost lesson): 'But JHWH is in his holy temple : be silent before
him all the earth'. Then follows :—

JHWH sat [enthroned or in judgement] at the Flood,
  JHWH sitteth as King for ever;
JHWH will give strength unto his people,
  JHWH will bless his people with peace.

What is meant by 'JHWH sat at the Flood'?[3] The late Dr.
Cheyne, regarding this reference to Noah's flood as impossibly
abrupt, translates 'At the storm [namely that described in the
Psalm] Jehovah sat enthroned'. But *Mabbul* is the technical
term for the great deluge and is used of no other tempest.
Dr. Cheyne overlooked the Pentecostal use of the Psalm. We
have in fact evidence dating from a century before our era for
associating the Feast with the covenant to Noah. The author of
the *Book of Jubilees* carried back the institution of the festivals

---

[1] The LXX title to the concluding ceremony of the Feast of Tabernacles
(ἐξοδίου σκηνῆς). The closing verses were chanted on New Year's Day.

[2] '*Gloria in excelsis* is the beginning and *pax in terris* the end,' Delitzsch
observes. But parallels suggest that the ' palace' of *v.* 9 is the heavenly, not
the earthly, temple.

[3] The LXX has 'will colonize (κατοικιεῖ) the flood', 'cause it to be inhabited'.
Cf. the Peshitta version ' will turn the flood' (sc. into dry land).

to patriarchal times. Pentecost, in his view, was the oldest of all. Having been observed in heaven since the creation, it was first kept on earth after the subsidence of the Flood. We read (vi. 15): 'And he gave to Noah and his sons a sign that there should not again be a flood on the earth. He set his bow in the cloud for a sign of the eternal covenant that there should not again be a flood on the earth to destroy it all the days of the earth. For this reason it is ordained and written on the heavenly tables, that they should celebrate the Feast of Weeks in this [the third] month once a year, to renew the covenant every year.' The writer clearly connected the Feast with the making of covenants; the covenant with Abraham is placed on the same occasion (xv. 1). He seems to have read *Shābuoth* 'Weeks' as *Shebuoth* 'Oaths', a confusion which we found also in Habakkuk. Thus the Deluge was associated with Pentecost already in the second century B.C., when the Psalter was being compiled, and the allusion to it in an appendix to this Psalm is not so incongruous as it seems.

In the body of the Psalm we may note the curious LXX rendering of *v.* 6. The Hebrew runs ' He maketh them (viz. the cedars of Lebanon) to skip like a calf, Lebanon and Sirion like a young wild-ox '. The LXX, reading the verb as רקק ' crush ' instead of רקד ' skip ', renders the first line καὶ λεπτυνεῖ αὐτάς, ὡς τὸν μόσχον τὸν Λίβανον, ' he shall pulverize them, even Libanus like the calf '. Probably the scene at Sinai is in the translator's mind and the golden calf which Moses burnt and ground to powder.[1]

PSALM LXVIII

On the great Whitsunday Psalm, *Exurgat Deus*, I have one comment to make in confirmation of a theory of its Maccabaean origin, and a few on details. We have rabbinical evidence for its allocation to Pentecost, but our main authority, the tractate *Sopherim*, ignores it. It was not the older of the Pentecost Psalms; it supplanted or supplemented Psalm xxix.

Some years ago, in a forcible article in the *Journal of Theological Studies*, Dr. C. J. Ball propounded a theory as to the event which this Psalm was written to commemorate.[2] He urged that it is all 'inspired by the rush and stir of contemporary life ' and

---

[1] Ex. xxxii. 20 רקד, Gr. κατήλεσεν αὐτὸν λεπτόν.

[2] *J. T. S.* xi. (1910) 415 ff. He had been anticipated by Wellhausen (Psalms, 1898, in *Sacred Books of O. and N. Test.*).

that it alludes to events—in particular a bringing back of Jewish exiles from the trans-Jordanic region—which cannot be identified with any of the great deliverances in the early history. 'The Lord said, I will bring back from Bashan' (*v.* 22) ; with which must be connected 'A mountain of God is the mountain of Bashan' (15) and the mention of Salmon (14) in the same locality.[1] In Dr. Ball's opinion the allusion is to an expedition of Judas Maccabaeus into the land of Gilead to rescue his compatriots who were threatened with extermination by their heathen neighbours.[2] The author of 1 Maccabees, where the story is found, proceeds to tell how the men of Ephron opposed the rescue party on their return and were defeated with such slaughter that the victors 'passed through the city over them that were slain', in literal accordance with the Psalmist's words 'that thou mayest dip thy foot in blood'. The victory was solemnly celebrated at the capital : 'And they went up to Mount Sion with gladness and joy, and offered whole burnt offerings, because not so much as one of them was slain.' Dr. Ball suggests that 'our Psalm or the first draft of it was the hymn composed for the festal service on this occasion'.

The point I would urge is the support given to this theory by a detail, strangely neglected by its author, in a second narrative of the same event. The writer of 2 Maccabees (xii. 31 f.), after describing the massacre at Ephron, goes on to say that the victors 'went up to Jerusalem, *the feast of weeks being close at hand.* But *after the (feast) called Pentecost* they marched in haste against Gorgias'. The celebration of the victory coincided with Pentecost. Dr. Ball, indeed, has a passing reference to that passage, but merely as giving an indication of the season of the year, in illustration of the 'bounteous rain' of the Psalmist. It is characteristic of the general neglect of Jewish liturgiology that he omitted to make further use of such strong corroborative evidence. The Psalm commemorates a double event, both the victory and the wheat-harvest. It is dominated by the two blending thoughts of Jehovah as God of battles and as giver of the land.

A few details may be added. The verse about the rain (9) is rendered in our Prayer Book version 'Thou, O God, sentest a gracious rain . . .', by the late Dr. Driver 'A bounteous rain thou didst shed abroad, O God'. Literally the words run 'A rain of freewill

---

[1] Salmon is probably the Jebel Haurān, the eastern frontier of Bashan and Gilead, known to Ptolemy as Ἀσαλμανός. References here and below are to the English verses.   [2] 1 Macc. v. 45 ff. (*c.* 164 B. C.).

offerings thou dost wave'.[1] The *Oxford Hebrew Lexicon* finds
the verb 'wave' 'not wholly suitable' and Lagarde emends it.
The festival use explains both the allusion to the rain and the
technical terms employed in both Hebrew and Greek. 'Thou
shalt keep the feast of weeks . . . with a tribute of a freewill
offering of thine hand', we read in the Deuteronomy lesson
(xvi. 10). This offering is to be waved by the priest as a תְּנוּפָה
or 'wave-offering' before the Lord, we read in the older
Leviticus lesson (xxiii. 20). The ceremony of waving, the
movement of the offering towards the altar and back, symbolized
its presentation to God and its return by Him to the priest. The
Psalmist acknowledges the gracious action of the Great High
Priest; His freewill offering of the rain alone makes possible
that of the worshipper. 'Of thine own have we given thee'.

The next verse (10), 'In thy goodness, O God, thou didst
prepare for the poor', seems reminiscent of the injunction in the
Leviticus lesson (xxiii. 22) to leave the gleanings of the harvest
for the poor and the stranger. Again, the sequence of ideas in
the earlier verses (4 ff.), 'His name is *JAH and exult ye before him.*
(5) A father of the *fatherless* and a judge of the *widows* is God in
his holy habitation (or "*place*", LXX τόπῳ). (6) 'God maketh the
solitary to dwell in a house; he bringeth out the prisoners into
prosperity', is the same as in the Deuteronomy lesson (xvi. 11 f.)
'And thou shalt *rejoice before JHWH* thy God, thou . . . and the
stranger and the *fatherless* and the *widow* that are in the midst
of thee, in the *place* which JHWH shall choose . . .; and thou
shalt remember that thou wast a bondman in Egypt'.

Reminiscences of Deut. xxxiii occur throughout the Psalm, but
here, as often, it is the conclusion which is most significant. In
the closing invitation to worship we have, as in Habakkuk, some
last echoes from the Blessing of Moses, but—and here lies the
interest—blending with them are phrases from Ψ. xxix. It was
fitting that the older Pentecost Psalm should supply the model
for the *finale* of its rival which was coming to supplant it in the
festival ritual. The verses run:—

Ψ. lxviii. 32 Sing unto God, O ye
kingdoms of the earth; O make
melody unto the Lord.

33 To him that rideth upon the heaven of heavens which are of old.	This is from Deut. xxxiii. 26 'Who rideth upon the heaven for thy help'.
Lo, he uttereth his voice, a mighty voice.	This is from Ψ. xxix. 4 'The voice of JHWH is with power'.

---

[1] וְשֵׁם נְדָבוֹת תָּנִיף, LXX βροχὴν ἑκούσιον ἀφοριεῖς.

Ψ. lxviii. 34 Ascribe ye strength unto God.,

His excellency is over Israel and his strength is in the skies.

35 Terrible is God out of thy sanctuaries.

The God of Israel, he giveth strength and mightiness unto the people. Blessed be God.

Again from Ψ. xxix (1) 'Ascribe unto JHWH glory and strength'.

Here we revert to Deut. xxxiii. 26 'Who rideth upon the heaven ... and in his excellency on the skies'.

And here to the final note of Ψ. xxix. (11), with *Benedictus* replacing *Benedicat*. His model runs 'JHWH will give strength unto his people; JHWH will bless his people with peace'.

LECTURE II (*continued*)

THE SEPTUAGINT AND JEWISH WORSHIP

(2) The Feast of Tabernacles

From the summer Feast of wheat-harvest I turn to the autumn vintage celebration—the Feast of *Sukkoth* or 'Booths'. 'Tabernacles' is perhaps too grandiose a term. Of immemorial antiquity, the feast is the earliest of which we have any historical record. Doubtless a heritage from the Canaanites, the cultus bears clear marks of its pagan origin. The Book of Judges ends with the incident of the yearly feast at Shiloh when the young women came out to dance in the vineyards.[1] That of Samuel opens with the annual pilgrimage of Elkanah to the sacrifice held at the same spot at the *Tekuphah*, the 'circuit' or revolution of the year.[2] This can be no other than that called by our oldest authorities, J and E, the Feast of Ingathering (*Asiph*) also falling at the *Tekuphah*.[3] The name Feast of Booths appears first in Deuteronomy and is retained in the later documents.[4] *Sukkah* is Isaiah's word for 'a booth in a vineyard',[5] and the feast probably took this title from the custom of the grape-gatherers of migrating, like the modern hop-pickers, to the scene of operations and camping under improvised shelters made of branches. The exile severed these agricultural associations, and the Priestly editors, finding the old meaning of *Sukkah* too homely or heathenish, interpreted it of the hut-dwellings during the wanderings in the wilderness.[6] Popular customs, however, refused to be suppressed, and a place was still found for what may be called the 'harvest-decorations' of the feast.[7] The practice, as we learn from the Mishna, was for the worshippers to carry in one hand *fasces* or *thyrsi*, known as *lulabs*, consisting of branches of palm, myrtle, and willow, while the other hand bore a citron. The booths, made of branches of the same trees, were also retained. Nehemiah records a great revival of the feast which had fallen into abeyance.[8]

---

[1] Judges xxi. 19 ff.   [2] 1 Sam. i. 3, 20 f.   [3] Ex. xxxiv. 22.
[4] Deut. xvi. 16, xxxi. 10; P and H. in Lev. xxiii.
[5] Is. i. 8.   [6] Lev. xxiii. 42 f.
[7] *ib.* xxiii. 40 H.   [8] Neh. viii. 14 ff.

One later celebration should be mentioned, the occasion when the officiating royal high-priest, Alexander Jannaeus, was pelted with the citrons for deviating from the established ritual at the water-libation;[1] the incident is a noteworthy illustration of the tenacity of time-honoured customs in the face of priestly opposition.   In New Testament times the feast, lasting seven days, with a closing and distinct ceremony on the eighth, was established as *the* great holiday season of the year. Jerusalem swarmed with pilgrims whose booths occupied every available corner of the city.

In its origin *Sukkoth* was the final harvest festival, marking the winding up of the agricultural year. But it was also the festival of the autumnal equinox. It was held, we are told, at the *Tekuphah*. *Tekuphah*[2] in Rabbinical Hebrew, and how much earlier we do not know, was the technical term for solstice and equinox. There were four *Tekuphoth*, of which that of the month Tishri was the third. Philo expressly states that the feast synchronized with the equinox.[3] The synchronism could only be approximate, as the Priestly editors employed the lunar month for their calculation. The solar reckoning, the *Tekuphah* of our oldest documents, seems likely to have been the more primitive.

For the *key-notes* of the festival we must look to the ritual; not to the sacrificial enactments of the Priestly Code, but to the popular ceremonies, which bring before us the two ideas which, we shall find, dominate the services : WATER and LIGHT. These ceremonies are the Water-drawing and the Illumination of the women's court of the Temple. Semi-pagan practices such as these are long-lived and doubtless reflect primaeval practice. The vivid accounts which have survived clearly come from an eye-witness, though the written record dates from after the year A.D. 70, which put an end once for all to the ceremonies described.

Of the *water-drawing* we are told[4] that a golden pitcher holding three *logs* (or pints) was filled with water from Siloam and borne in procession through the Water-gate, with blowing of trumpets and the singing of Isaiah's words 'Therefore with joy shall ye draw water out of the wells of salvation',[5] up to the Temple. There, with a libation of wine, it was poured by the priest, in the

[1] Jos. *Ant.* xiii. 13. 5 (372).
[2] Apparently connected with the verb *nakaph*, 'go around', which is used of the annual 'round' of the feasts in Is. xxix. 1.
[3] καιρὸν ἔχουσα τὸν μετοπωρινῆς ἰσημερίας De spec. leg. ii. (de Septen.) 204 (24).
[4] T. B. *Sukkah*, iv. 9.   [5] Is. xii. 3.

sight of all, into two pipes beside the altar; through these it passed underground to the valley of the Kidron. The ceremony was repeated each day of the feast.

We are not left to conjecture as to its meaning. In its far-off origin it symbolized the rainfall of the coming year; it was, it seems, a species of rain-charm. The Jews themselves virtually so explained it, though more spiritual meanings were found. 'Offer ye waters before me on the Feast of Sukkoth that the rains of the year may be blessed to you', so the Talmud.[1] The festivals looked forwards as well as back; thanksgivings for blessings received mingled with prayers for future mercies. At each festival the destiny of the succeeding season was fixed. At Passover judgement was passed on the wheat-harvest, at Pentecost on the fruit-trees, at Tabernacles on the water.[2] Prayers for rain began at this season.[3] A striking picture of the struggle for water, in which the city has been engaged throughout its history, has been drawn by Sir George Adam Smith.[4] The pool itself, from which the procession started, commemorated a notable achievement in this age-long contest with nature, viz. the construction by Hezekiah of the conduit by which the waters of the only spring in the neighbourhood were diverted within the walls. 'He made the pool and the conduit and brought water into the city.'[5] The ceremony of the water-drawing prefigured a time when the need for this extraneous supply would cease, and waters would issue from beneath the very threshold of the Temple, a river to make glad the city of God.

Of the other ceremony, the all-night *illumination* of the women's court of the Temple and the accompanying torch-dance, we have an unusually vivid description.[6] It was regarded as an integral part of the day-time proceedings, being known as the 'House' (that is the indoor portion) 'of the water-drawing'. We read of the great candelabra with wicks made of cast-off priestly vestments and with four ladders to each on which stood young priests replenishing the oil; 'and there was not a court in Jerusalem that was not lit up by the light of the house of water-drawing.' But the most significant part of the programme was the procession

[1] T. B. *Rosh hash.*, 16 a.   [2] *ib.* i. 2.   [3] T. B. *Taanith*, i. 1.

[4] *Jerusalem*, i. 122. He remarks how the 'innumerable cisterns, public and private, prove very distinctly that the people of Jerusalem have always depended for their water, *in the main*, upon the collection and storage of the rains and the surface percolations'.

[5] 2 Kings xx. 20.   [6] T. B. *Sukkah*, v. 2–4.

of priests at the close just before dawn. 'At the upper gate stood two priests with trumpets in their hands. *When the cock crew* they blew a blast, a long note and a blast. This they repeated on reaching the tenth step and again on entering the court. And so they proceeded sounding the trumpets until they reached the east gate. At the east gate they turned their faces from east to west and said : "Our fathers who were in this place turned their backs on the Temple and their faces towards the east and worshipped the sun towards the east; but we, our eyes to JAH ". R. Jehuda says : They repeated again and again, " We belong to JAH and raise our eyes to JAH ".'

So with a solemn, public disclaimer of sun-worship the ceremony ended at cock-crow. Surely this is very significant and justifies the belief that the Illumination is another relic of nature religion. The disclaimer is based on Ezekiel's vision of the sun-worshippers in the Temple,[1] which might account for the place at which it was pronounced. But why at this season, at this particular hour of cock-crow, heralding the rising sun at the equinox ? The whole picture is that of a pagan carnival thinly veiled under priestly influences.[2] The illuminations, I have no doubt, commemorate the autumnal equinox ; they mark the beginning of the descent to the long winter nights, and were in their origin a charm or prophylactic against the encroaching powers of darkness.

First the rain-charm, then the sun-charm. We seem to be carried back to a primitive Canaanitish ' Feast of the sun and the rain ', the two factors, under God, in the ripening of the harvest. The dominant ideas of the nature religion were, of course, spiritualized, notably by the author of the 42nd Psalm ; of the wealth of new meaning put into them by one Visitor to the feast I shall have occasion to speak.

Zechariah XIV

I turn to the prophetical lessons and Psalms. Of the former our oldest authority[3] names two, Zechariah xiv and 1 Kings viii (the dedication of Solomon's temple). I will take first the

---

[1] Ez. viii. 16.

[2] We read of feats of jugglery. 'Rabban Simeon b. Gamaliel ... would take eight torches in his hands and throw them into the air and catch, and one would not touch another.'

[3] T. B. *Meg.* 31 a.

Zechariah lesson, then the appointed Psalms, and finally the alternative *Haphtarah*.

As the *Haphtarah* for Pentecost was the last chapter of Habakkuk, so that for Tabernacles was the last of 'Zechariah'. Both chapters are foreign to their contexts. The last six chapters of Zechariah are notoriously an appendix to the prophecy and the last of all may once have had an independent existence.[1] The LXX here affords little assistance, but, excepting two verses, the text presents no serious difficulty. The points I would emphasize are two: (1) the prominence given not only to the festival, which is expressly named, but to its dominant *motifs*; (2) the close connexion with the festival Psalm, for which the lesson provides the model.

Beside the joy of the water-bearing the autumn festival had other, more solemn, associations. The Jews connected the final harvest of the year with a harvest in the future—an ingathering of the nations to Judaism in the days of Messiah. This ingathering was, however, to be preceded by a combined assault of the nations, 'Gog and Magog' as they are called, upon the chosen people. It is this world-battle and its sequel which the lesson depicts.

We are told of the mustering of the armies against Jerusalem, the capture and looting of the city, and the deportation of half the inhabitants. Then and not till then does JHWH intervene, descending on the Mount of Olives, which at the touch of His feet is rent by an earthquake, to do battle with the enemies of Zion. The writer passes to the blessings of the millennium thus ushered in: continuous daylight (according to the restored text), a perennial issue of living waters flowing down on either side of Jerusalem, the city renovated and enlarged. He then reverts to the fate of the belligerent nations, gloating over the horrible plague wherewith JHWH will smite them and their beasts of burden. A remnant, however, will embrace Judaism. The verse (16) which links the lesson both to the festival and, as will be shown, to the festival Psalm must be quoted. 'And it shall come to pass, that every one that is left of all the nations which came against Jerusalem shall go up from year to year to worship the King, the LORD of hosts, and to keep the feast of tabernacles.' Then mark the penalty for disobedience (17): 'And it shall be, that whoso of (all) the families of the earth goeth not up unto Jerusalem to worship the King, the LORD of hosts, *upon them*

---

[1] It deals at greater length with the topics of chap. xii, of which it is in a sense a 'doublet'.

there shall be no rain.' Refusing to keep the harvest-festival
they shall have no harvest; the rain unprayed for shall be
withheld. For rainless Egypt a special punishment, not clearly
defined, is reserved.[1] The chapter ends with prosaic ceremonial
details. So vast will be the concourse of worshippers that every
pot in Jerusalem will be requisitioned for sacrificial use.

Perpetual daylight and an unfailing water-supply; those,
with the absence of winter, are the outstanding blessings of the
millennium. The verses (6 f.) about daylight have unfortunately
reached us in a corrupt form and appear to state the very
opposite, viz. that there will be a weird day of gloom (neither
day nor night) with light at evening time.[2] I follow the
interpretation of Professor Mitchell in the *International Critical
Commentary*: 'There shall be no more cold and frost (the "cold
and frost" we owe to the LXX); it shall be one day (that is,
one *continuous* day), not day and night (alternating)', to which,
to make his meaning unmistakable, the writer adds, 'Yea, at
eventide there shall be light'. This interpretation has the
support of Jerome, whose commentary is valuable from the
knowledge shown of Jewish exegesis. 'Dies', such is his paraphrase, 'dies in qua non succedent lux et tenebrae, sed erit
lumen perpetuum.' The cessation of winter is twice adumbrated
in the LXX, in the allusion to cold and frost already mentioned
and in the next verse (8), where in the phrase 'in summer and
winter shall it be', the translators substitute 'spring' for 'winter',
and Jerome infers the abolition of the latter.[3]

An unfailing water-supply and perpetual daylight inevitably
recall the Water-drawing and the Illumination. Nor can we fail
to note with reverence that it is just these two ideas—Water
and Light—which the greatest Visitor to the feast, fastens on
and applies to Himself. 'Now on the last day,' we read in the
fourth Gospel, 'the great (day) of the feast (i.e. the seventh day,
known as the Great Hosanna), Jesus stood and cried saying,
If any man thirst, let him come unto me, and drink. He that
believeth on me, as the scripture said, out of his belly shall flow
rivers of living water.'[4] 'Again therefore Jesus spake unto

[1] The Targum supplies the obvious penalty: 'The Nile shall not rise for
them'.
[2] An interpretation which led to the use of the passage on Good Friday in
early Christian lectionaries.
[3] 'Hoc dicamus quod illo tempore non sit hiems sed ver aestasque perpetua.'
[4] John vii. 37 f.

them, saying, *I am the light of the world*: he that followeth me shall not walk in the darkness, but shall have the light of life.'[1] That these profound sayings were prompted by the festival cultus has often been suggested. That the first of them is probably an allusion to the Zechariah lesson has been acutely conjectured by Dr. Israel Abrahams.[2] 'As the scripture said, out of his belly shall flow rivers of living water.' We search the Scriptures in vain for the actual words, but in all probability they are to be explained as a paraphrase of the Zechariah passage 'Living waters shall go out from Jerusalem '(*v.* 8), for the synagogue reader might substitute for the name of the Holy City the pseudonym by which it was affectionately known, the *ṭabūr* or 'navel'. Like Delphi to the Greek, so Jerusalem to the Jew was the ὀμφαλός or centre of the universe.[3]

Psalm LXXVI

From the special lesson I turn to the special Psalm (lxxvi 'In Judah is God known') named by our main authority, the treatise *Sopherim*;[4] and I would propose to study it as the Jewish worshipper read it as a companion to the lesson. It falls symmetrically into four stanzas of three verses each, the first and third stanzas terminating with Selah. The final stanza, in Dr. Briggs' opinion, is a later addition, one of those semi-liturgical appendices by which a Psalm is sometimes accommodated to a particular occasion. The gloss is for us the most interesting portion.

The scene is, as in the lesson, Jerusalem a battle-field. The Psalm commemorates some signal intervention of God to deliver the Holy City from an enemy at the gate. 'At Salem is his tabernacle . . . there brake he the lightnings of the bow, the shield, the sword, and the battle.' The doughty foes sleep their

---

[1] John viii. 12.

[2] *Studies in Pharisaism*, i. 11. For other explanations, see the *Expositor*, vol. xx (1920), p. 385 (Prof. Burney); *ib.* p. 196 (Dr. Rendel Harris).

[3] The idea was based *inter alia* on Ez. xxxviii. 12 (a chapter closely allied to Zech. xiv) where Gog purposes to turn his hand against the people that dwell in the navel of the earth. Cf. the central position of Jerusalem in mediaeval maps.

[4] xix. 2.

last sleep; the would-be spoilers are spoiled and paralysed; chariot and horses share their riders' fate. The Psalmist sees in the stricken field the hand of God alone. The fame of the deliverance has carried His name far and wide in Israel.

Rarely is it possible in the Psalter to identify with certainty allusions to historic events later than the occupation of Canaan. Here there is a general consensus of opinion, ancient and modern, that the scene portrayed is the destruction of Sennacherib's army. This interpretation goes back to the Greek translators who appended to the title the words 'touching the Assyrian'. I do not question that verdict; the writer undoubtedly had that occasion in mind. But the Psalm must also be read, in the light of the lesson, of the coming Armageddon. We trace in the text a tendency to project into the future the details of the historic deliverance under Hezekiah. The destruction of Sennacherib's army served as the model for the picture of the final overthrow of Gog and Magog. The same metaphor is used of Gog in Ezekiel, 'I will turn thee about and put hooks into thy jaws',[1] as of Sennacherib in Kings, 'I will put my hook in thy nose and my bridle in thy lips, and I will turn thee back by the way by which thou camest'.[2] The historian's veiled allusion to the fate of the Assyrian host 'when the Angel of Death spread his wings on the blast' was materialized into the loathsome plague described in 'Zechariah'. In a remarkable, perhaps post-exilic, passage attributed to Isaiah, the song celebrating the Assyrian's downfall is likened to the chant used on the inaugural night of a feast. Picturing the exultation over the deliverance, the prophet writes: 'A song shall there be for you *as in the night when a feast is consecrated* (or " opened") and joy of heart like his who marches with a flute to come into the mount of JHWH . . . For through the voice of JHWH shall Asshur be panic-stricken'.[3] The Feast, as usual when undefined, must mean the Feast of Tabernacles; and we have allusions here both to the water-bearing procession to the Temple mount to the accompaniment of flute-playing,[4] and to the midnight inaugural ceremony. It seems that even at the comparatively early date when these words were written the festival opened

---

[1] Ez. xxxviii. 4.
[2] 2 Kings xix. 28 = Is. xxxvii. 29.
[3] Is. xxx. 29, 31.
[4] 'The pipes at the time of water-drawing were played sometimes on five days, sometimes on six', says the Mishnah (T. B. *Sukkah*, v. 1).

with nocturnal rites, at which a song was chanted reminiscent of the signal deliverance from Assyria.

Turning to details, the title tells us of a long history; the Psalm had figured in many anthologies before being incorporated in our Psalter. It is interesting to note that in the 'middle Greek period' (c. 250 B.C.) it was set to stringed instruments and stood in the collection of the Chief Musician, where it had for companion with the same setting the Pentecostal Psalm of Habakkuk.

Verse 2 runs in the R. V. 'In Salem also is his tabernacle and his dwelling in Zion'. The Hebrew for 'his tabernacle' is סֻכּוֹ, which is rather 'his covert' or 'lair'; and as the second noun may bear a similar meaning,[1] the late Dr. Driver renders 'In Salem also is his covert and his lair in Zion'. JHWH is likened to the lion of Judah. Since this metaphor seems to be resumed in *v.* 4 ('mountains of prey') and finds a parallel in Isaiah's allusion to Sennacherib,[2] it is probable that it stood in the original Psalm. On the other hand, *Sukkoh* 'his covert' is hardly distinguishable from *Sukkah* 'a booth' or *Sukkatho* 'his booth'. Hence other modern commentators render 'his pavilion' (Kirkpatrick) or 'his bower' (Cheyne), and the ancients (Greek, Syriac, and Midrash) did likewise. The word 'tabernacle' of our English Bible happily recalls the thought which could not fail to occur to every pilgrim at the Feast of Booths. JHWH is present with His worshippers, Himself observing the feast in the immemorial fashion; He too has His *Sukkah* in the Holy City.[3] The Greek translator here writes ὁ τόπος αὐτοῦ, a euphemism for 'His booth'; in the other festival Psalm (xlii. 4, Gr. xli. 5) he uses the two words ἐν τόπῳ σκηνῆς. The *Sukkah* or Booth of God is a remarkable phrase only found in these two Psalms and in one other which there is reason to connect with this feast (xxvii. 5); it is not to be confused with his *Ohel* or Tent, which is much more frequent.[4]

Verse 3 'There shattered he the *Reshephs* (the winged missiles) of the bow'. If Sennacherib's host perished at some distance

---

[1] The two occur in juxtaposition in Job xxxviii. 40 (of young lions).

[2] Is. xxxi. 4.

[3] The Midrash on the passage runs: 'R. Berechia has said, In the beginning of the creation of the world the Holy One, blessed be He, made Himself a booth in Jerusalem, in which, if one may so speak, He prayed.' The Hebrews did not shrink from these bold anthropomorphisms.

[4] The distinction is lost in the English and, in part, in the Greek; these versions employ 'tabernacle' and σκηνή indiscriminately.

from the city, Zion was invariably the scene of the final world-battle. The B text of the LXX adds an explicit reference to the crushing of the last enemies, ἐκεῖ συνκλάσει τὰ κέρατα; a clear case of history merging into apocalypse.

The second stanza opens with the verse (4) quaintly misrendered in our Prayer Book, 'Thou art of more honour and might than the hills of the robbers'. The Hebrew has 'Illumined (or "radiant" נָאוֹר) art thou, majestic, from the mountains of *Tereph*' (usually rendered 'prey'). The Greek φωτίζεις σὺ θαυμαστῶς ἀπὸ ὀρέων αἰωνίων.

'Radiant', 'light-bringing'. We have one of the *motifs* of the festival.[1] It seems almost wanton to emend so apposite and symbolical a word. Yet it has been proposed[2] to transpose the radicals and for נָאוֹר to read נוֹרָא 'terrible', because that word opens the third stanza and occurs at the close of the fourth. The suggestion, it is true, has the support of Theodotion (φοβερός), and the parallelism is in its favour; the Psalm is unusually symmetrical. If the Psalmist wrote 'terrible', 'illumined' or 'light-bringing' is part of the accommodation to the feast which seems to have affected the whole Psalm from the first.

'Majestic'; Heb. אַדִּיר, Gr. θαυμαστῶς. The Hebrew word had special associations with the feast. The Greek translator found it along with a mention of the *Sukkah* in the other special Psalm.[3]

For 'mountains of *Tereph*' (or 'prey') the Greek has 'eternal mountains'. Dr. Briggs acutely accounts for the divergence by assuming an original reading עַד which might bear either sense 'eternity' or 'prey'. We cannot determine what the Psalmist wrote; 'mountains of prey', carrying on the lion metaphor of *v.* 2, is likely to be right. But we may try to put ourselves in the place of the worshipper at the feast, and I cannot but think that he would, in the light of the lesson, read another meaning into the verse. He would identify the mountains from which JHWH radiates forth with the Mount of Olives on which 'his feet shall stand in that day'.[4] He would

---

[1] Augustine, with the Latin version of the LXX before him, and interpreting it in a Christian sense, seems to see the sun of righteousness rising over the eastern mountains. 'The great mountains are the first to receive thy light, and from thy light which the mountains receive the earth also is clad. But the great recipient mountains are the Apostles, who received as it were the first beginnings (*primordia*) of the orient light.'

[2] So Cheyne and, doubtfully, Driver.

[3] xlii (xli). 5 ἐν τόπῳ σκηνῆς θαυμαστῆς. Cf. also Is. xxxiii. 20 f.

[4] Zech. xiv. 4.

know the word *Tereph* (from the root meaning 'pluck' or 'tear')
in its other sense of a fresh pluckt leaf, and associate it with
the cognate adjective *Tārāph*, which, in its only occurrence in
Scripture, denotes a fresh pluckt *olive* leaf.[1] 'Mountains of
plucking' would for him connote 'leafy mountains' or more
specifically 'mountains of olive leaves'. It would be a readily
intelligible synonym for the mount from which he had gathered
olive branches for his *thyrsus* and his booth. One translator
in fact interpreted the phrase on these lines; Theodotion writes
'from the fruitful mountains.' (ἀπὸ ὀρέων καρπίμων).

The next two verses (5 f.) portray the spoiler spoiled and
chariot and horse 'fallen into a dead sleep'. Both pictures find
parallels in the Zechariah lesson and its prototype, Ezekiel's
vision of Gog.[2] The lesson expressly mentions the beasts as
sharing their riders' fate.

The third stanza (the rising of God to judgement to save the
afflicted of the earth) calls for no remark. With it, in Dr. Briggs'
opinion, ended the original Psalm.

The parallels between Psalm and Lesson, so far cited, may by
themselves appear inconclusive. To clinch the connexion, to
establish that the former was in fact interpreted in the light
of the latter, we turn to the added stanza in its Greek dress.
Verse 10 runs in the Prayer Book version :—

> The fierceness of man shall turn to thy praise :
> and the fierceness of them [an ancient misprint for ' other ']
> shalt thou refrain.

The Hebrew, in Dr. Driver's version, runs :—

> For the wrath of man shall give thanks unto thee ;
> with the residue of wraths *thou wilt gird thyself* (תַּחְגֹּר).

The words have proved a *crux* to interpreters ; ' the whole
verse is dark ', wrote Dr. Cheyne. But if we turn to the Greek
we find :—

> ὅτι ἐνθύμιον ἀνθρώπου ἐξομολογήσεταί σοι,
> καὶ ἐνκατάλιμμα ἐνθυμίου ἑορτάσει σοι.

'The residue of brooding wrath *shall keep feast to thee*.' The
translators, instead of תַּחְגֹּר read the word, almost indistinguishable from it in the unvocalized text, תְּחָגֶּךְ.[3] The *hag* intended
must be the pre-eminent Feast of Tabernacles, and we at once
recall the Zechariah lesson : 'And it shall come to pass, that
every one that is left of all the nations which came against

---

[1] Gen. viii. 11.   [2] Zech. xiv. 14 f. ; Ez. xxxix. 9 ff.
[3] Or (less probably) תָּחֹג לְךְ.

Jerusalem shall go up from year to year to worship . . . and
to keep the feast of tabernacles.'[1] Here surely we have the
key to the stanza appended by some early worshipper. 'The
residue of wraths (that is, of the wrathful nations) shall keep
the Feast of Tabernacles in Thy honour.' In the *Haphtarah*
from Habakkuk we found lectionary references to the first lesson;
here we have an allusion to the second lesson embedded in the
Psalm.

The verse exemplifies the supreme value, on occasions, both
of the Greek version and of the liturgical factor in Biblical
interpretation. An otherwise obscure allusion finds a simple
explanation in the arrangements of the Jewish Church calendar.
We may infer that before the date of the LXX Psalter, at least
as early as 100 B.C., Zechariah xiv and Psalm lxxvi were
companion pieces, used at one and the same service. If the
connexion were forgotten or severed (and a substitute for the
Psalm was found ere long) the Hebrew text represented by the
LXX would cease to be intelligible and invite emendation.

The remainder of the stanza summons Israel to pay its vows
and the neighbouring nations to bring presents to the Fearful
One (the Arch-Fear) who lops off the spirit of princes and is
terrible to the kings of the earth. The vows and presents may
have their festal connexions;[2] but the interesting word here
is בָּצַר 'lop off'. It is the technical term for gathering grape
clusters and forms a final link with the festival of the Vintage
(בָּצִיר).[3]

PSALMS XLII–XLIII

The tractate *Sopherim* names no rival to Psalm lxxvi. In the
modern service, usually conservative, its place has been taken
by a pair of Psalms, originally one, xlii and xliii. There are
many reasons for regarding this alternative as based on ancient,
if not quite the most ancient, practice. (i) The use is common
to the ritual of the two main divisions of orthodox Jews,
Ashkenazim and Sephardim.[4] The divergence of these groups

---

[1] Zech. xiv. 16.

[2] The vows possibly allude to the private offerings of certain first-fruits which
began at this feast and continued to the next (T. B. *Bikkurim*, i. 6). The presents
recall the sequel to the Chronicler's story of Sennacherib (2 Chron. xxxii. 22 f.).

[3] Cf. Judges ix. 27; and for the Divine Husbandman, John xv. 1 f.

[4] Oesterley, *Psalms in Jewish Church*, 165, 167. The Ashkenazim assign xlii
to the first, xliii to the second, day of the feast; the Sephardim employ both
at all services.

takes us far back and a community of practice is proof of antiquity. (ii) The use of the pair of Psalms carries us yet further back. The original unity of the pair is shown by the absence of a title for xliii and the refrain which they have in common, ' Why art thou so cast down, O my soul ? ' The modern practice seems to be older than the separation ; yet the Psalm is already divided in the LXX. (iii) Lastly, the festival use has left its impress on the Greek, the Midrash, and apparently even the original text.

The Psalm is a moving lament of a priest or Levite, looking back from his banishment in the upper Jordan region towards the Holy City, with a passionate longing for its services, and a lively recollection of its festal processions at which in happier days he took a leader's part. The autumn festival is specially in mind. He touches all the key-notes.

The Psalmist gives expression in their most spiritual form to the thoughts associated with the water-bearing. ' Like as the hart desireth the water-brooks, so longeth my soul after thee, O God. My soul is athirst for God, for the living God : when shall I come and see the face of God ? ' He uses the recognized phrase for visits to the Temple at the pilgrim festivals. ' My *tears* have been my food day and night ' ; the sustenance of the living waters being denied him.

Then in *v.* 4 (5) comes the thought of the processions. The Hebrew in the Revisers' rendering runs : ' These things I remember, and pour out my soul within me, | How I went with the throng and led them to the house of God, | With the voice of joy and praise, a multitude keeping holyday.' The Greek translators read otherwise and in one particular perhaps rightly, viz. in their mention of the *Sukkah*, God's Booth or Tabernacle. For ' with the throng ' (בַּסָּךְ, a word without Biblical parallel) they read בְּסֹךְ or בְּסֻכָּה ' in a booth ' ; also, less happily, for אֲדַדֵּם ' I used to lead them in a solemn procession ', אַדֶּרֶת ' majestic ', while the frequentative imperfect becomes a future ; the whole phrase thus running ' For I shall pass along in [or " to "] the place of a marvellous tabernacle unto the house of God '.[1]

---

[1] The Midrash (tr. Wünsche) understands the booth to be a portable conveyance used by the pilgrims. ' They went up to the feasts ', writes this early commentator, ' to see thy face in litters (or " sedan-chairs ", σκεπαστής) made in the manner of a booth.' This same commentator finds another very curious reference to the water-bearing in this verse. On the phrase הָמוֹן חוֹגֵג he

At *v.* 7 with the sense of his loss the waters for which he pines take a more formidable shape. 'Deep calleth unto deep [1] at the sound of thy waterspouts.' [2] In place of 'the waters of Shiloah that go softly', from whose pool he once led the procession, he sees only roaring cataracts threatening to engulf him. 'All thy breakers and billows have gone over me.' The words, both in Hebrew and Greek, recur *verbatim* in the Prayer of Jonah, the lesson for the Day of Atonement. [3] The Psalmist can echo the words of the Fast-day and wear the sackcloth (or, as the Greek has it, the heavy countenance) befitting it; the joy of the succeeding festival is not for him.

Such are the echoes of the daylight ceremony. Of the nightly illuminations we may perhaps find two traces: 'And in the night his song shall be with me' (xlii. 8), and again 'O send out thy *light* and thy truth; let them lead me: let them bring me unto thy holy mount, and to thy dwelling-places' (xliii. 3). We leave the exile peering into the darkness, from the Hermons or Mount Mizar, straining his eyes to see the glare which lit up every court in Jerusalem, his ears to catch the notes of the Levites' song.

Psalm CXVIII

There remains yet one Psalm intimately connected with the feast, at which I can but glance. This is cxviii, the last component of the Hallel. The Hallel was sung at all the great festivals, but this concluding Psalm held a special place in the ritual of *Sukkoth.* [4] In the interpretation of one verse the LXX again comes to our aid.

The Psalm is designed to be sung antiphonally by a procession approaching the Temple and by the Levites who respond

goes out of his way to assert that the participle חוֹגֵג ('on pilgrimage', 'keeping holy-day') is a Greek word and means 'a conduit' (*Wasserleitung*). Apparently he connected it with ἀγωγός or ὑδραγωγός and had in mind either the water-bearers or Hezekiah's conduit which fed the pool whence the procession started.

[1] The Midrash refers these words to the upper waters addressing the lower waters and generally to the rain-fall.

[2] It is interesting to note that the word צִנּוֹר ('water-pipe' in the P. B. version) in its only other occurrence in the Old Testament (2 Sam. v. 8 'Whosoever smiteth the Jebusites, let him get up to *the watercourse*') probably refers to the perpendicular shaft discovered by Sir C. Warren leading directly from the Virgin's spring into the city. See Driver, *in loc.*   [3] Jon. ii. 3.

[4] And is commonly believed to have been composed for the great celebration of the feast recorded in Nehemiah.

from within. In the body of it the reiterated reference to a ring
of enemies, 'All nations compassed me round about' (v. 10 ff.),
should be read in the light of the final world-contest of the
Zechariah lesson, 'I will gather all nations against Jerusalem
to battle'. But it is the concluding verses, sung as the procession enters the Temple and bringing us into close touch with
the ritual, with which I am concerned.

The chorus without raise the cry of Hosanna: 'We beseech
thee, O JHWH, save now (הוֹשִׁיעָה נָּא) ; we beseech thee,
JHWH, send us now prosperity.' The Levites within reply
'Blessed be he that entereth in the name of JHWH; we bless
you from the house of JHWH'. The procession respond, according to the Revisers' version (v. 27), 'The LORD is God, and he
hath given us light:[1] bind the sacrifice with cords, even unto
the horns of the altar'. Ritual and vocabulary alike condemn
this rendering. The victim was not, to our knowledge, bound
to the sacred altar-horns; there is no sure warrant for rendering
חַג 'a festal sacrifice'; the preposition עַד is an impossible
substitute for לְ after the verb 'bind'. The late Dr. Driver's
translation, 'Bind the festal victim with cords (and lead it)
unto the horns of the altar', removes two of these difficulties
but retains the unusual meaning for חַג. Now the Mishna tells
us[2] of a procession with palm-branches which was made round
the altar each day of the feast and repeated seven times on
the last day, with cries of 'We beseech thee, JHWH, save now,
we beseech thee, JHWH, send now prosperity'. It adds that
the branches were shaken[3] at the 'Hosannas' as also at the
closing refrain 'O give thanks unto JHWH'. So closely, indeed,
were the wands associated with the cries of 'Save now' that
they came to be known as 'Hosannas'. To this practice there
is a clear allusion in the Greek of v. 27 which in place of
'Bind the *Hag* with cords' has συστήσασθε ἑορτὴν ἐν τοῖς
πυκάζουσιν, 'Set in order (marshal) a (or "the") festival with
the overshadowing (or "leafy") (branches)'. That the translators are right in their rendering of עֲבֹתִים ('leafy branches', not
'cords') appears from the Levitical prescription in which the
cognate adjective (עָבֹות) is used: 'And ye shall take you on

---

[1] Note again the dominant *motif* of the feast.

[2] T. B. *Sukkah* iv. 5-7.

[3] Was this in origin a water-finding charm? Note Aquila's equation of
הדר = הידור = ὕδωρ in Lev. xxiii. 40 (*ap.* Field's Hexapla). The trees to
be employed were 'water-trees' (? as divining rods).

the first day ... boughs of leafy trees.'[1]   Their interpretation of
אָסַר 'bind' as 'begin' or 'marshal' is unusual, but justified by
its use with מִלְחָמָה for 'to begin battle'. They give *ḥag* its
natural meaning; but the Hebrew word is probably here used
in what some scholars regard as its original sense, a procession
in a circle.[2]

In the latest English version of the Old Testament,[3] the
learned Rabbis of America have been the first to adopt the
LXX reading: 'Order the festival procession with boughs, even
unto the horns of the altar.' Following the lead of another
great American scholar, Dr. Briggs, I would go further and
treat the words as a liturgical direction which has crept from
the margin into the text. They overweight the verse, and the
balance of clauses is improved by their absence. We then read:

JHWH is God and hath given us light: [*Here start the
branch-waving procession.*]
  even unto the horns of the altar.

In other words, He has by some dazzling display of light
manifested his acceptance of the sacrifices upon the altar. We
recall how at the dedication both of the Tabernacle and, according to the Chronicler, of Solomon's Temple, there came
forth fire from the LORD and consumed the burnt-offerings and
the sacrifices.[4]

1 KINGS VIII

This brings me to my final passage. For to the other associations of the feast there was added the commemoration of the
dedication of the Temple. An alternative *Haphtarah* to the
Zechariah lesson was found in 1 Kings viii, which was read in
two portions on different days of the feast.[5]

The interest of the chapter, from the liturgical standpoint,
lies in (1) the opening and closing verses, and (2) the stanza
of poetry which is put into Solomon's mouth, and the editorial
revision to which these portions have been subjected.

I must pass over the opening and closing verses. The LXX
here presents a shorter text than the Hebrew; commentators
are agreed that the additional Hebrew matter comes from a late

---

[1] Lev. xxiii. 40.
[2] Cf. חוג 'encircle' and Driver, *Notes on Hebrew text* on 1 Sam. xxx. 16.
[3] Philadelphia, Jewish Publication Soc. of America, 1917.
[4] Lev. ix. 24, 2 Chron. vii. 1; cf. 2 Macc. ii. 10.
[5] T. B. *Meg.* 31 a.

editor. I suspect the longer opening to be a sort of lectionary proem, analogous to the short introductory clauses prefixed to some of the Gospels in the English Book of Common Prayer.

The main interest lies in Solomon's canto. A comparison of Hebrew and Greek shows that the passage has been drastically edited, as regards both text and position. In the Hebrew the words are placed early in the chapter (*v.* 12 f.), immediately after the descent of the cloud upon the house, an incident which, in the editor's mind, they are clearly intended to illustrate. The text runs :—

> Then spake Solomon :
>   JHWH hath said that he would dwell in the thick darkness.
>   I have surely built thee a house of habitation,
>   a place for thee to dwell in for ever.

In the Greek the words occupy a later position (*v.* 53 b) after the prayer of dedication. Another line is prefixed to the canto and the source from which it is taken is named at the close. The Greek, though obviously by an unintelligent translator, brings us nearer to the original than the M. T., and runs as follows :—

> Then spake Solomon concerning the house when he had finished building it:
>   The sun hath the LORD made known (*v.l.* 'placed') in heaven ;
>   He has said that he will dwell in (*v.l.* 'out of') thick darkness.
>   Build my house, a splendid house for thyself,
>   to dwell upon newness.
> Behold is not this written in the Book of the Song?

I cannot dwell on the history of the interpretation of this celebrated passage. I can but summarize the main conclusions I have reached; I have given a fuller statement elsewhere.[1]

The Book of the Ode (הַשִּׁיר) is doubtless identical with the primitive collection of national songs elsewhere called the Book of Jashar (הַיָּשָׁר). The last line of the stanza (Gr. 'to dwell upon newness') is, I suggested, in reality no part of the poem, but a final docket; as in the Psalm of Habakkuk a rubric has been incorporated into the text. A common origin for the obviously edited Hebrew '*A place for thee* to dwell in for ever' and the Greek τοῦ κατοικεῖν ἐπὶ καινότητος can be found in a title 'For the sabbath, on (or "set to") Alamoth', that is 'for soprano voices'.

In the opening line of the Greek canto we have mention of

---

[1] *J. T. S.* xi. (1910) 518 'New light on the Book of Jashar'.

the sun: 'The sun hath the LORD made known (ἐγνώρισεν) in
heaven.' Professor Burkitt has conclusively shown[1] that the
easier Lucianic reading ἔστησεν must be rejected, that ἐγνώρισεν
is what the translator wrote and that it represents a Hebrew
הוֹדִיעַ. But הוֹדִיעַ cannot be right. What verb stood in the
original Hebrew? Professor Burkitt suggested an imperative of
הוֹפִיעַ 'shine':

> Sun, shine forth in the heavens;
> JHWH hath said He will dwell in darkness.

I ventured to suggest, with the duplication of one letter,

> The sun of glory is beclouded in the heavens;
> JHWH hath said He will dwell in darkness.

This calls up a picture of a solar obscuration peculiarly in
keeping with the associations of the feast of the autumnal
equinox, when the hours of darkness begin to encroach upon
the day.

Certainty in restoration of this kind is rarely attainable. For
our immediate purpose two results seem to emerge. (1) The
nucleus of this lesson was probably a song. The *Haphtarah*
grew out of a canticle. (2) The song began with some statement
about, or invocation to, the sun, the exact nature of which is
doubtful. Whatever that statement was, later editors thought
good to excise it, together with the mention of the semi-pagan
song-book from which the canto was drawn. Editors and
translators realized well enough the Jew's besetting temptation,
among heathen neighbours, to sun-worship, and were suspicious
of passages, especially in the mouth of a polytheist like Solomon,
where the sun was placed in juxtaposition or comparison with
JHWH. Thus, in Ps. lxxxiv (Gr. lxxxiii) 12, the Alexandrians
scented danger in the innocent words 'For the LORD God is
a sun and shield' and freely paraphrased 'For the LORD God
loveth mercy and truth'.[2] In the present instance, the drastic
action of the editors is intelligible if, rightly or wrongly, they
saw in the canto a relic of paganism and read it as a solar charm
or invocation for the feast of the equinox. I find in their
expurgation a striking parallel to the explicit disclaimer of
sun-worship at the close of the Illumination ceremony: 'Our
fathers in this place worshipped the sun towards the east; but
we, our eyes are to Jehovah.'

---

[1] *J. T. S.* x. (1909) 439 'The Lucianic text of 1 Kings viii. 53 b '.
[2] Perhaps selecting ἔλεος from its resemblance to ἥλιος.

But I would rather close with words which, though now abandoned in óur services, the fathers of some of us used to chant at evensong on this very day of Advent[1] at the turn of the year—the *Teḳuphah*—'O dawning brightness of the ever-lasting Light and Sun of righteousness: come and illumine those who sit in darkness and in the shadow of death!'

[1] This lecture was delivered on the evening of December 20. The Antiphon quoted is from the 'O Sapientia' series.

LECTURE III

THE SEPTUAGINT AND JEWISH WORSHIP:

(3) The Book of Baruch and the Fast of the Ninth of Ab

In the preceding lecture I endeavoured to show that the use of the Old Testament in Jewish worship is an important factor in the interpretation of select passages. To-day I take as my subject a book, the whole structure and framework of which seems to be governed by liturgical considerations. I dealt then with two of the principal festivals and the canonical Scriptures employed thereon; my lecture to-day will relate to a Lenten season and a book which never obtained admission to the Hebrew canon.

The Book of Baruch, though one of the shortest, is not the easiest of the deutero-canonical writings. Absent from the Hebrew and relegated in our English Bible to the Apocrypha, it held in the Greek Bible a more honourable position. There it forms, along with the Lamentations and the so-called Epistle of Jeremiah, the first of a trilogy of writings appended to the book of that prophet. That it stands first, taking precedence of Lamentations, is remarkable; the disciple above the master, the secretary before the seer. But, indeed, it seems from the first to have been treated in the Greek Bible rather as an integral part of the prophecy than as an independent work; the Fathers from Irenaeus onwards cite it as 'Jeremiah', and as far back as we can trace its history it, or some part of it, formed an inseparable adjunct to the prophecy.

The structure of the book is not clearly indicated in our English Apocrypha. It consists of two distinct portions, the first half being written in prose, the second half in the style of Hebrew poetry; each of these again falls into two subdivisions. 'The common theme', as Mr. Harwell[1] writes, 'which binds the two parts together is the destruction of Jerusalem and the exile of her children.' We have (1) the historical introduction with the express statement that the book is intended for liturgical use

---

[1] *The Principal Versions of Baruch* by R. R. Harwell (Yale University, 1915).

(i. 1–14) ; (2) a long confessional prayer of the exiles (i. 15–iii. 8). To these prose sections, without any formal connexion, are appended (3) a poetical homily on Wisdom (iii. 9–iv. 4), and (4) a series of cantos of consolation (iv. 5–v. 9).

Setting aside the historical preface, we have three sections with the topics Penitence—Wisdom—Consolation. Each of these sections is largely dependent on different parts of the Old Testament. The penitential section is in bulk a mosaic from Daniel and Jeremiah ; the Wisdom section is based on Job and other sapiential books ; the Consolations are drawn from deutero-Isaiah, the typical comforter, as Jeremiah was the typical censor, of the Jewish nation. The Confession lacks literary merit, except such as it derives from the borrowed passages ; the poetical portions are not such slavish imitations of their models, and in places almost attain to the level of the best parts of Jewish literature.

I was first attracted to the Book of Baruch by a minor problem as to its literary connexion with the Greek Jeremiah. But in the course of my researches this interest was absorbed by a discovery which, I venture to think, sets the whole book in a new light. The book is expressly designed for use in the Lord's house on certain days not clearly defined (i. 14), and it can only be fully understood in the light of that statement. It is strange that this clue has not been followed up. Ewald stands almost alone in emphasizing this purpose ; but, beyond suggesting that ' the days of season ' (or ' assembly ') refer to the sabbaths,[1] he did not attempt to connect the book with any particular occasion.

I find the clue to the days intended in the structure of the work, with its three well-marked divisions with the topics Confession—Wisdom—Consolation. Now this is not a purely heterogeneous collection of ideas. The triad Confession (or Punishment)—Wisdom—Comfort meets us elsewhere. In a tractate of the Talmud [2] we find the Hebrew kings and prophets, the wise men, the Hagiographa, and so on arranged in groups of threes typifying these or kindred ideas. The ideas exemplified are normally Punishment, Wisdom, Piety, but in the group of

---

[1] Quoted by Kneucker, *in loc.* Cf. *Hist. of Israel* (E. T.), vol. V. 208, n. 2 'In the three divisions of its own contents the whole book thus supplies a type of the contemporary worship in the house of prayer : first prayer, next preaching, and lastly a more elevated prophetic close '.

[2] T. B. *Berakoth*, 57 b.

F

Prophets Comfort replaces Piety, and we have the three topics of
our book: Punishment (typified by Jeremiah), Wisdom (by
Ezekiel), and Comfort (by Isaiah). In Baruch the confession is
largely drawn from Jeremiah, the consolations from Isaiah; the
wisdom section, for reasons which will appear, is based, not on
Ezekiel, but on the sapiential books. This sequence of ideas,
from Punishment through Wisdom to Consolation, seemed so
fitting that some rabbis arranged the prophetical books in the
corresponding order: Jeremiah, Ezekiel, Isaiah.[1]

Now this same *catena* of ideas reappears in a series of sabbaths
associated, like our book, with the destruction of the Temple.
The Jews brought back from Babylon the custom of annual fasts
at fixed dates. Before the exile fasts were exceptional, and only
held on extraordinary occasions.[2] The post-exilic fixed fast-days
took two forms. On the one hand was the great Day of Atonement, the ceremony of purification held at the opening of the
year and intimately connected with the New Year Feast. On
the other hand, and earlier than the Day of Atonement, which is
unrecorded in Ezra, we find mention of four fast days commemorating the outstanding national calamities at the time of
the Babylonian capture. We learn from Zechariah that these
four fasts, held in the fourth, fifth, seventh, and eighth months,
existed in his time,[3] and that at least two of them had been
observed throughout the exile. 'When ye fasted and mourned
in the fifth and in the seventh (month), even these seventy years,
did ye at all fast unto me?'[4] The principal fasts were that of
the fourth month (Tammuz), commemorating the capture of the
city, and that of the fifth month (Ab), recalling the culminating
disaster—the burning of Temple and city by Nabuzaradan.
Traditions varied as to the exact dates of the capture and
conflagration; a variation due in part to later attempts to
produce a fictitious symmetry with corresponding events in
the Roman siege. The conflagration is variously placed on
the 7th, 9th, and 10th of Ab; but the anniversary of this
blackest of days was always kept on the 9th. With the return
from exile and the rebuilding of the Temple the fast lost its full
significance, and a deputation waited on Zechariah to inquire
whether the mourning of the fourth month should be continued.[5]
For the subsequent history of the fast we are without information

---

[1] T. B. *Baba Bathra*, 14 b.

[2] Wellhausen, *Proleg. to Hist. of Israel*, 111.

[3] Zech. viii. 19.   [4] *ib.* vii. 5.   [5] *ib.* vii. 3.

until some six centuries later an overpowering stimulus to its renewal was given when Herod's Temple suffered the same fate as Solomon's at the hands of the Romans. It was probably about this time, in the years following A.D. 70, that the 9th Ab became the centre of a cycle of sabbaths, which linked it on the one side to the Fast of Tammuz, on the other to the autumn New Year.

The Jewish summer, the period from Pentecost to Tabernacles, was barren of feasts and full of mournful associations. Within this season fell three of the 'national calamity' fasts and the Day of Atonement. *Rosh Hashanah*, the Feast of the New Year, from its close association with the latter, hardly broke the continuity of this long Lenten season. Now these fast-days came to be linked up together by a chain of sabbaths having the 9th of Ab for pivot. We might compare our succession of Sundays named after Trinity; or, as the pivot here occupies a middle position and the sabbaths on either side differed in their character, we should speak more correctly of a Lenten season of sabbaths before the 9th Ab and an Advent season of sabbaths after it. The cycle began with the 17th Tammuz, the reputed date of the Babylonian capture of the city. Between that date and the 9th Ab, the date of the burning of the Temple, fell three Punishment sabbaths (*Straf-sabbate*), on which, according to our main authority, lessons were read taken respectively from the first and second chapters of Jeremiah and the first of Isaiah. The black fast-day of the 9th Ab was followed by a period of seven Consolation sabbaths (*Trost-sabbate*), which looked forward to and bridged the interval to the New Year. On these were read passages of consolation taken from deutero-Isaiah. Subsequently, at some date later than any with which we are concerned, two more sabbaths were added which carried on the series to the Day of Atonement.[1]

Our main authority for this cycle is the so-called *Pesikta* (or Book of Selections) of Rab Kahana. That work consists of homilies on the lessons, from Law or Prophets, selected for use on the principal feasts and fasts in the Jewish calendar and on two groups of sabbaths, the Ab group of ten sabbaths already

[1] Like our 'Stir-up' Sunday, these were known from the passages read as 'Seek (ye) sabbath' (from Is. lv. 6) and 'Turn sabbath' (from Hos. xiv. 1 (2)). The complete cycle thus embraced (1) three sabbaths of Punishment, (2) the fast of 9th Ab, (3) seven sabbaths of Consolation, and subsequently (4) two more Lenten sabbaths in preparation for the Day of Atonement.

mentioned, and a smaller group of four with the Feast of Purim for pivot. The homilies take for their text a verse or two at the beginning or end of the respective lessons. The *Pesikta* is ranked by some critics among the oldest Midrashim which we possess; it is at any rate based on very ancient materials. The portion embracing the cycle of ten sabbaths, which opens with a reference to R. Abba bar Kahana, is thought to have been the oldest nucleus and to have given its name to the whole. The cycle seems to have had a considerable vogue in early times, but to have afterwards dropped out of general use. The *Pesikta* was for a long time lost, and only rediscovered in the nineteenth century, the *princeps editio* being dated 1868.[1]

Now the three main portions of our book curiously conform to this cyclical arrangement. Both cycle and book have as their cardinal theme the burning of the Temple. Answering to the three sabbaths of Punishment with lessons (for at least two of them) from Jeremiah, we have in *Baruch* a penitential section in three portions, also largely based on Jeremiah. The central or Wisdom section of the book I assign, for reasons which will appear, to the Fast itself. Corresponding to the seven sabbaths of Consolation we find a final consolatory section divided into seven minor portions, based on deutero-Isaiah and, to a large extent, on the particular passages which were read on those sabbaths. The connexion is clearest in this final section. My discovery, if it be one, of the liturgical framework of the book began here. So close a parallelism, in the general scheme and in particulars, can hardly be fortuitous. I am inclined to regard our book as, in a sense, an unsuccessful rival to that which follows it in the Greek Bible—the Book of Lamentations, a work which through the ages has been linked with the 9th of Ab, has formed the model for a series of beautiful dirges (*Kinoth*) for that day, and was itself not improbably actually composed for such liturgical use.

The discoverer of a new line of interpretation is unfortunately not absolved from the task of dealing with other problems presented by his text and with the work of his predecessors.

---

[1] Ed. S. Buber; I have not had access to this. I have used the German translation of Wünsche (Leipzig, 1885), Zunz, *Die gottesdienstlichen Vorträge der Juden* (Frankfurt a. M. 1892), and Dr. B chler's article on ' The Triennial Reading of the Law and Prophets' in the *Jewish Quarterly Review*, vol. vi. 1894, pp. 62–73.

Brief reference is necessary to modern literature, ancient versions, and some outstanding problems.

We possess useful English editions in Archdeacon Charles' *Apocrypha* and in the *Speaker's Commentary*; but as the fullest and most comprehensive exposition that of Kneucker, produced as long ago as 1879, still holds the field. Kneucker's work is a monumental example of German thoroughness and industry ; his judgement is perhaps more open to question. It has been challenged in one particular by the latest writer, Mr. Harwell, of Yale University, in his dissertation on *The Principal Versions of Baruch* (1915). The main service of Mr. Harwell's work is that he has established the importance of the Old Latin version known as *b*. Of the two Old Latin versions one, *a*, which is incorporated in the Vulgate (though Jerome had no hand in it), has hitherto been regarded as older than *b*, which is printed beside it in Sabatier. The superiority of *b* is inferred by Mr. Harwell from its shorter text, from the absence of 'doublets', and chiefly from the fact that it begins with Jer. lii. 12 (the burning of the Temple by Nabuzaradan), i. e. it is 'based upon a Greek text in which Baruch has not yet been separated from Jeremiah'. In his opinion the Old Latin *b* is descended from a pre-Origenic text which antedates the standard text contained in all our Greek MSS.[1]

Beside the two Latin versions we have a pair of Syriac versions. The Syro-hexaplar so called (the seventh-century Syriac rendering of the LXX column in Origen's *Hexapla*) is important because of its reference to a Hebrew original. Three notes state that certain words are 'not in the Hebrew'. Notwithstanding these notes, a colophon adds that the whole book was 'obelized', in other words, that Origen knew of no Hebrew when he compiled the *Hexapla* in the third century. The Hebrew original must have been lost at an early date. The Syro-hexaplar further contains interesting lectionary marks indicating the beginning and end of lessons read in the Syrian Church services.[2] Though older than the Syro-hexaplar, the other Syriac version, the Peshitta, is inferior. It abounds in conflate readings, and bears at least one mark of Christian influence. Both Syrian versions possess an interest as emanating from the only country from which we have evidence for the use of the book in the *Jewish* services. All the ancient versions seem to have been made from the Greek, none from the lost Hebrew.

[1] *op. cit.*, pp. 41 f., 44, 51.　　　　[2] *ib.* 7.

Brief as it is, the book presents several unsolved problems. Opinions are divided on such questions as its unity, the language in which it was first written, its date or the dates of its component parts. A *unity* of design in the mind of the final editor may be inferred from its apparent relation to the sabbath cycle already mentioned; but behind this unity are indications of compilation from diverse sources. The work is clearly composite. The prose and poetical portions come from different hands. The divine titles afford a convincing criterion. Κύριος (Lord) occurs abundantly (about forty times) in Part I (down to iii. 8), never in Part II, which employs instead ὁ αἰώνιος, ὁ ἅγιος, and θεός.[1] This diversity in style is accompanied by a diversity in tone, a difference of attitude towards Israel's oppressors. In Part I the exiles exhort their brethren in Jerusalem to 'pray for the life of Nabuchodonosor king of Babylon, and for the life of Baltasar his son'; Part II on the contrary contains the fiercest imprecations upon the foreign foe. There are indications that the two poems come from a single hand; there are also links between the two prose portions. This composite origin may be variously explained. Mr. Harwell regards the poems as the older material, which an editor has incorporated, prefixing the less original prose sections of his own composition. I am not convinced by this, and incline to the older view that the prose portions are the original work which has subsequently been amplified by the addition of the poems. I find it harder to believe that a writer with the conciliatory tendency shown in the Introduction incorporated and endorsed the final invectives, than that a later editor by appending the cantos gave a more vindictive turn to a prose work which he appropriated entire. As to *language*, it is generally agreed that Part I had a Hebrew original. This appears not only from the notes in the Syro-hexaplar 'not in the Hebrew',[2] but from the occurrence in the Greek of phrases which can only be accounted for as mistaken renderings.[3] Whether Part II also had a Semitic original is more doubtful. Both Kneucker and Harwell have reproduced a Hebrew text of this portion, and the latter writer claims to have proved that the first poem was composed in three-beat and the latter in five-beat measures.

[1] In Part I θεός is practically confined to the combination Κύριος ὁ θεός.

[2] Which have been explained away. Nestle held that 'the Hebrew' did not refer to Baruch but to the Old Testament passages which form its model.

[3] In particular 'Hear the prayer of *the dead* Israelites' (iii. 4), where מְתֵי 'men of' has been read as מֵתֵי 'the dead of' (Israel).

I am not competent to judge whether he has proved his case; but, as has often been remarked, Part II presents the general appearance of being an original Greek composition,[1] and this view is supported by the apparent dependence of the second poem on the *Greek* Psalter of Solomon. As regards the Greek and its relation to the translation of Jeremiah I have reluctantly abandoned my former view.[2] The Greek, I now think, is all by a single hand. The similarity in Part I to the style of the second translator of Jeremiah is due to a close imitation of his style, and is insufficient to prove that the translations were made by one and the same man.[3] The question of *date*, especially of the date of Part I, is difficult to determine. Outside limits are given on the one hand by the dependence of Part I on the Book of Daniel, on the other by the earliest citations of the book by Christian writers of the second century; but those limits leave a rather wide range of 300 years (150 B.C. to A.D. 150). The main problem is whether the whole or either part is later than A.D. 70. My own opinion is that the whole work is not earlier than the first century of our era. Part I was written in Hebrew not long before A.D. 70; after the stirring events of that year the book was reissued in Greek in an enlarged form, with the addition of Part II. The fierce invectives and the call for reprisals in the latter part can refer, I think, only to the Roman conquerors. I shall revert to this question in connexion with the Historical Introduction. I do not claim to have solved these riddles, and have considerable hesitation in suggesting so late a date for Part I. I have one new contribution to make to the interpretation of the book. For the rest, indeed for the whole, I speak under, and shall welcome, correction. My theory is based on the final edition of the work, and is unaffected by the history of any earlier stages through which it may have passed. The external evidence, slight but significant, for the actual use of the book in Jewish worship, I reserve to the end. My theory as to the use for which it was *designed* stands or falls on its own merits, and is not touched by that evidence. The design perhaps never was carried out in its entirety.

I proceed to examine the several portions of the book.

[1] One phrase near the close, ὡς θρόνον βασιλείας v. 6, meaning apparently 'as on a royal throne', suggests, but does not, I think, absolutely necessitate a Hebrew original, as Archdeacon Charles holds (*Apocr. and Pseud.* i. 573).

[2] In *J. T. S.* iv. 261.

[3] Part II of Baruch shows a few links with 'Jeremiah β'; note in particular χαρμοσύνη iv. 23.

The Historical Introduction

The Introduction (i. 1–14) states that the book was written by Baruch in Babylon in the fifth year, on the seventh day of the month, at the season when the Chaldaeans captured and burnt Jerusalem. The date is extraordinarily vague. The starting-point from which the fifth year is reckoned is not stated; the month is not named, though the day of the month is; the capture and burning of Jerusalem appear to be regarded as contemporaneous, though actually separated by an interval of three weeks. The reference to the burning on the seventh day of the month can, however, only refer to the fifth month of Ab, on the seventh of which, according to the account in Kings,[1] the conflagration took place. The words 'in the fifth month' have possibly dropped out after 'in the fifth year'. Anyhow the book was ostensibly written in the early years of the Judaean exile in Babylon. It was read in the ears of the captive king Jeconiah and his countrymen, who wept, and fasted, and prayed. A money collection is then made and sent to the remnant at Jerusalem with a covering letter enjoining them to expend it on offerings to be presented on the altar· of the Lord (represented as still standing), with prayers 'for the life of Nabuchodonosor king of Babylon, and for the life of Baltasar his son, that their days may be as the days of heaven above the earth',[2] that so the exiles might find favour and live peaceably under Babylonian rule. 'And pray for us also . . . for we have sinned.' The letter proceeds (i. 14): 'And ye shall read this book which we have sent unto you, to make confession in the Lord's house, upon a (or "the") feast day and upon days (or "the days") of season.' Then follows the Confession.

I need not dwell on the inaccuracies which make it impossible to accept this record as authentic. Baruch was never, to our knowledge, in Babylon; the last we hear of him in the Book of Jeremiah is that he was forced to accompany the prophet into Egypt, where he probably ended his days.[3] A more serious objection is the mention of Nebuchadnezzar and Belshazzar his son as contemporaries. The writer here, as in the subsequent Confession, follows the Book of Daniel, and follows it in a notorious error. Inscriptions prove that Belshazzar was not

---

[1] 2 Kings xxv. 8; in Jer. lii. 12 f. 'the tenth'. This dependence on 2 Kings suggests that Jeremiah still lacked the Historical Appendix (chap. lii) when 'Baruch' was attached to it.

[2] Cf. Deut. xi. 21.   [3] Jer. xliii. 6 f.

the son of Nebuchadnezzar and was never king of Babylon.
This dependence on Daniel at once brings Part I of our book
down to Maccabaean times.

What, then, does this Introduction tell us as to the real
purport of the book? It is, as I read it, a recommendation from
a community of the Jewish Dispersion to their brethren at
Jerusalem to do two things: (i) to pray for the civil rulers of
a foreign country (called 'Babylon'); (ii) to adopt the use of
certain liturgical forms and ceremonies which they observe themselves. These two petitions require consideration.

(i) *The prayer for foreign rulers.* The Introduction as a whole,
and this request in particular, are clearly based on Jer. xxix
(xxxvi). 1 ff. In Baruch we read 'And these are the words of the
book, which Baruch wrote . . . in Babylon', and lower down
'Pray for the life of Nabuchodonosor and his son'. In Jeremiah
we have 'And these are the words of the book which Jeremiah
sent from Jerusalem unto the elders of the captivity', followed
by the advice (*v.* 7) 'Seek the peace of the land (Heb. 'city')
whither I have caused you to be carried captive, and pray unto
the LORD for it; for in the peace thereof shall ye have peace'.
That is the model. 'Settle down', says Jeremiah, 'in Babylonia
and do not look for a restoration to your country until after
seventy years'. In Baruch we have, as it were, a rejoinder from
the exiles to the Jews at Jerusalem to put into practice themselves the pacific policy recommended by Jeremiah.

Such a rejoinder or retort might conceivably be romance pure
and simple, without ulterior motive; but is more likely to have
an underlying object arising out of contemporary circumstances.
These *pseudepigrapha* usually have a purpose. What are the
circumstances here referred to? Now if we abandon, as we
must, the period of the Babylonian captivity, it is difficult to
find any intervening occasion forming a suitable background
until we come down to the great war with Rome of A.D. 66-70.

An attractive theory has been propounded that Babylon here,
as in the Apocalypse, stands for Rome, and that Nabuchodonosor
and Baltasar are no other than Vespasian and Titus. The theory
is attractive because we learn from Josephus that the abandon-
ment of the customary sacrifices for the Emperor was the *fons et
origo belli.* 'Eleazar, son of Ananias the high priest,' he writes,
'a very daring youth, being then the captain [of the Temple],
persuaded those who officiated in the Temple services to accept

no gift or sacrifice from a foreigner. This action', he continues, 'laid the foundation of the war with the Romans; for they thereby abrogated the sacrifice on behalf of that nation and the Emperor.'[1] This affords a striking illustration to Baruch's advice, 'Pray for your rulers'; and, though this brings the date of our book down as late as A.D. 69 (when Vespasian became Emperor), I am tempted to accept the theory in so far as to regard Nabuchodonosor and Baltasar as pseudonyms for the Roman generals.

I am not, however, prepared to follow Kneucker in the equation of Babylon with Rome *as the place of writing*. All indications suggest an eastern, rather than a western, origin for our book.

(1) The cycle of sabbaths, forming, as I believe, the framework of our book, has no known early connexion with the West. Opinions are divided as to whether it originated in Babylon [2] or Palestine;[3] no one associates it with Rome. The *Pesikta* is traced either to Palestine or more probably to some community of the Diaspora in the neighbourhood of Palestine.[4] (2) Again, our book shows acquaintance with Palestinian literature of the first century of our era. Use is made of the Greek Psalter of Solomon which was probably produced in Palestine in early New Testament times; also of a version of Daniel allied to that of Theodotion and to the text cited by New Testament writers. (3) Lastly, the only known record of the liturgical use of our book comes from the region of Syria and Mesopotamia.[5]

For these reasons I should look for the place of origin to the region north of Palestine, to Syria or perhaps Mesopotamia, on the eastern fringe of the Roman Empire. I should read this Introduction as an eirenicon put out from this quarter about A.D. 69, when the sacrifices for the Emperor had been abandoned and the siege of Jerusalem was impending, to the effect 'Don't provoke further disaster; resume your former practice and pray for the lives of our rulers and yours, the Romans'. In his Introduction to his *Jewish War*, Josephus tells us of the ferment in this region at the outbreak of hostilities. 'The whole of the Eastern Empire', he writes, 'was in the balance; the [Jewish] insurgents were fired with hopes of its acquisition, their [Roman] oppo-

---

[1] Jos. *B. I.* ii. 409 (xvii. 2). See Schürer, *Hist. of Jewish People*, ii. 1. 302 ff., where references are given for the daily sacrifices for the Roman authorities.

[2] 'Probably', Elbogen, *Der jüd. Gottesdienst*, (1913) p. 178.

[3] So apparently Büchler, *J. Q. R.* vi. (1894) pp. 63, 72.

[4] Zunz, *Die gottesdienstl. Vorträge der Juden*, 207, note *a*.

[5] See below, pp. 107 ff.

nents feared its loss. For the Jews hoped that all their fellow-countrymen beyond the Euphrates would join with them in revolt.'[1] These hopes at that time proved barren; on the contrary, if I read our book aright, the Eastern Jews counselled submission. On the other hand, in the later revolt under Trajan in A.D. 116, it was just these Jews of the Diaspora in Mesopotamia who, with the homeland, played the leading part.[2] The second edition of our book, with its vindictive ending, appeared, I believe, in the interval between the two outbreaks.[3]

(ii) *The suggested liturgical use.* The exiles make a second request to the mother-country, viz. to read the book which accompanies their letter on certain occasions not clearly defined. We have in another apocryphal book a parallel for an epistle from one Jewish community to another commending the adoption of certain ceremonial practices. In the second book of Maccabees the Jews of the capital exhort their brethren of Alexandria to keep the newly-instituted Feast of Dedication.[4] Here the order is reversed, and it is the province which presumes to dictate an innovation to the metropolis.

Verse 14 runs 'And ye shall read this book which we have sent unto you, to make confession (ἐξαγορεῦσαι) in the house of the Lord, upon a (or " the ") feast day and upon days of occasion (ἐν ἡμέρᾳ ἑορτῆς καὶ ἐν ἡμέραις καιροῦ)'.[5] Two occasions for the reading are specified: a feast and a series of days of meeting or solemn assembly not ranking among the feasts.

The versions present two variants. As a curiosity we may note in passing the text of the Peshitta Syriac. This Syrian translator misread καιροῦ as Κυρίου and rendered ' on a fast-day or on the Lord's days'. He was obviously influenced by the custom of his native Church; the other Syriac version, the Syro-hexaplar, indicates the length of the Christian lessons from this book.

Far more important is the variant reading of the old Latin b:

---

[1] *B. I.* i. 4 f. (Proem 2).

[2] Mommsen, *Provinces of Rom. Emp.*, ii. 221 ff.

[3] It was for the benefit of ' the natives of upper Syria ' that Josephus composed the original Aramaic edition of his *Jewish War* (*B. J.* I. *ad init.*). The narrative may have had an incendiary effect, undreamt of by its author.

[4] 2 Macc. ii. 16 ' Seeing then we are about to keep the purification, we write unto you ; ye will therefore do well if ye keep the days'. Cf. i. 18.

[5] The Hebrew was doubtless בְּיוֹם חָג וּבִימֵי מוֹעֵד.

'et legetis librum quem misimus ad vos in domo domini *in die sollemni.*' This translator omits both the word 'to make confession' and the words 'and on days of occasion'.[1] The book is to be read only 'on a solemn day'. Influenced by Mr. Harwell's defence of the shorter Latin text, I was strongly tempted to find in this reading a trace of the first edition of our book, and to hold that it was intended for use only on the 'feast' or 'solemn day', and that the words 'and on days of occasion' were inserted in the enlarged edition. On further consideration I doubt the originality of the *b* text. There are other examples in this Old Latin version of omission of obscurities or studied brevity,[2] and I believe this to be one. I should be much more inclined to regard the Latin text as original, were it not that it further omits ἐξαγορεῦσαι, 'to make confession'.

For ἐξαγορεῦσαι strictly applies only to Part I of our book, the Confession which immediately follows. It is not applicable to the Homily and the Consolations. In this word I think we *may* find a witness to a first edition ending at iii. 8, a relic which escaped revision when the text was enlarged. The word is unlikely to have been inserted at a later stage, when Confession formed the smaller portion of the book. The Old Latin seems to have omitted it on this very ground.

The reading is to take place 'in the Lord's house'. Notwithstanding the opening reference to the Chaldaean conflagration, the Temple is therefore represented as still standing, although, as would appear from the following Confession, in a sorry condition: 'Thou hast made the house which is called by Thy name as it is this day' (ii. 26).

'On a feast day and on days of season.' I will take the 'days of season' first. I assume that definite days are intended and that the words are not, as has been suggested to me,[3] comparable to the phrase 'and on such other days as the Ordinary shall appoint'. Does the book enable us to identify the season? Only one season is specified, namely in *v.* 2 'the season when the Chaldaeans took Jerusalem and burnt it with fire'.[4] That

---

[1] The omissions are shared by the Ethiopic version (frankly an epitome), which goes further still in omitting 'which we have sent unto you'.

[2] e.g. ii. 18 (Λ ἐπὶ τὸ μέγεθος ὃ βαδίζει κύπτον καί), iii. 1 (Λ ἀκηδιῶν); for brevity, ii. 23 (Λ φωνήν *bis*).

[3] By my friend the Rev. C. S. A. Whittington.

[4] The καιρός in iii. 5 (the only other occurrence of the word) doubtless bears the same meaning.

surely is the occasion intended. According to the traditional
reckoning the city was taken on the seventeenth of the fourth
month Tammuz;[1] the burning of Temple and city occurred three
weeks later, on the 9th of Ab. I conclude that these three weeks
are the καιρός of *v.* 14. The book in its older form was to be read
on a feast day, and on the three sabbaths intervening between the
17th Tammuz and the 9th Ab. The Punishment sabbaths, in
Dr. Büchler's opinion, were instituted first, before the sabbaths
of Consolation.[2] The word מוֹעֵד (here rendered by καιρός) in
later Hebrew was specially used of the fast of Ab.[3] In the
enlarged *Baruch* καιρός would cover the whole cycle including
the Consolation sabbaths; no revision would be necessary. I have
no doubt that in the final edition the καιρός meant the complete
cycle.

Can we identify the other occasion, the feast-day, on which
the book was to be read? We might expect mention to be made
of a Fast-day rather than of a Feast; but ἑορτή (or חַג) will not
bear that sense, nor can the vaguer *dies sollemnis* of the Old Latin,
in view of its use elsewhere to render ἑορτή, be adduced as proof
of any variant in the Greek. Though *v.* 14 in our text specifies
no feast, it has been thought that it did once name a date, which
has got out of place in a MS. written in double columns
and is to be found in *v.* 8. In that verse, which betrays its nature
as a gloss by its lack of cohesion with the context, we are told of
the return of certain vessels to Jerusalem on the tenth of the
month Siwan. This date is again absent from the Old Latin *b*,
while the Syriac has the important variant 'on the 10th of Nisan'.
Commentators accordingly transpose this date from *v.* 8 to *v.* 14,
which then runs 'Ye shall read this book on the 10th Siwan, on the
feast day, and on days of season'; which they interpret to mean
'on the Feast of Pentecost and the fast days which followed it'.
I should agree that the date in *v.* 8 has got out of place, but in
view of the evidence of the versions I should banish it altogether
from the original text. The '10th Siwan' and the '10th Nisan'
are alternative glosses, guesses at the particular occasion which
the writer left undefined.

What was that occasion? There is little to be said for Pentecost, which normally fell on the 6th (not the 10th) Siwan; of the
fast days following it I can find no record.

[1] According to 2 Kings xxv. 3, Jer. lii. 6, on the 9th Tammuz.

[2] *J. Q. R.* vi. 64.

[3] Levy, *Neuhebr. und Chald. Wörterbuch, s. v.*

The answer is not so obvious as in the case of the days of season. Yet if there was one *ḥag* more appropriate than another to this solemn Confession, it was that of the New Year. New Year's Day (*Rosh hashanah*) was, in fact, the one day in the Jewish calendar which could rank alike as feast and fast. Opinions were divided on the question whether it should be reckoned 'a good day' (a יום טוב) or not; ultimately the view prevailed that its penitential character, as a day of judgement, outweighed its festal associations.[1]

But, in the light of the misplaced Syriac gloss in *v.* 8 'on the 10th Nisan', I would venture to go further. The feast which this community of the eastern Dispersion wish to recommend to the mother-country is not that which the Palestinians themselves observed at the autumn or civil New Year, but the old Babylonian feast of the *spring* New Year held at the beginning of Nisan. We shall find that our book was, in fact, read by the Syrian Jews at that very season. Among the Babylonians the feast *par excellence*, of remote antiquity, was that of the spring New Year held during the first eleven (or more) days of the month Nisan.[2] The Jews, apparently on the return from exile, imported this feast, with some of its associations, into their own calendar; with the distinction that they transposed it to the autumn. While the 1st Nisan was regarded as the opening of the ecclesiastical year, the Jewish New Year's Day Feast was kept on the 1st Tishri. It is, however, not unlikely that the eastern Dispersion would retain the custom of their adopted country and wish to commend it to their Palestinian brethren. The suggested prayer for royalty favours this identification. At the Babylonian feast the fate of the king's life was determined for the coming year.[3] The associations of the Jewish *Rosh hashanah* were largely influenced by those of the Babylonian feast. The New Year *Haphtarah* (the Song of Hannah) and the New Year Psalms attest a connexion between the day and the destiny of the civil ruler.[4] What more natural than that the Jews of the eastern Dispersion should invite their Palestinian brethren at the spring New Year to pray for the life of their rulers? The petition may have had a liturgical, as well as a political, motive.

[1] Elbogen, *Der jüdische Gottesdienst*, p. 146.
[2] M. Jastrow, *Religion of Bab. and Assyria*, 1898, pp. 676–82.
[3] See e.g. Schrader, *Keilinschriften*[3], 370 f., 514 f. ; Jastrow, *op. cit.* 680.
[4] See the writer's article 'The Song of Hannah and ... the Jewish New Year's Day' in *J. T. S.* xvi. 177 ff.

THE CONFESSION

I have necessarily dwelt at some length on the Introduction; the Confession which follows (i. 15–iii. 8) may be lightly passed over. As shown in Dr. Swete's text, it falls naturally into three parts: (1) the Confession proper (or תּוֹדָה, i. 15–ii. 10) beginning 'To the Lord our God belongeth righteousness, but unto us confusion of face'; (ii) the prayer for mercy (תְּהִנָּה, ii. 11–35) 'And now, O Lord, thou God of Israel'; and (iii) a final prayer (iii. 1–8), gathering up in more informal and personal style the ideas of the previous sections, beginning 'O Lord Almighty, thou God of Israel, a soul in anguish and a weary spirit crieth unto thee' and ending on the note 'Though penitent, we are still in exile'. The whole is a mosaic of Old Testament reminiscences. The groundwork of the first two sections is the confession in Daniel (chap. ix) in a version resembling that of Theodotion; interwoven with this are fragments of the Greek Jeremiah, in a style closely akin to that of the second of the two translators of that book.

We cannot directly connect the three portions of the Confession with the particular lessons from Jeremiah and Isaiah traditionally assigned to the three *Straf-sabbate*. But the traditional lessons are not necessarily the oldest. We shall find a much closer connexion between the final portion of our book and the lessons for the *Trost-sabbate*. Here I would merely urge that the three-fold division readily lends itself to the cycle arrangement, one section being allocated to each of the sabbaths.[1]

THE HOMILY ON WISDOM

I pass to the second half of the book, and first to the Homily on Wisdom (iii. 9–iv. 4), penned, as I shall endeavour to show, as a sermon for the 9th of Ab.

The abrupt transition in the Greek from Confession to Homily is bridged in the Old Latin *b* by a sentence which suggests that this translator may have known of the existence of the Confession as a separate book: 'Et cum explicuisset *librum orationis captivorum*, accipiens spiritus vocem Ierusalem loquutus est dicens', &c. The book of the exiles' prayer is ended; the spirit hears and responds to the city's cry.

---

[1] If, with Mr. Harwell, we regard the shorter text of the Old Latin in i. 14 as original, the Confession was designed in the first edition for use only on the feast-day; the adaptation to the cycle was an afterthought.

'Hear, O Israel,' begins the preacher, 'commandments of life:
give ear to understand wisdom.' The opening words recall the
Shema' (Deut. vi. 4) with which it was customary to preface
a discourse in the synagogue on solemn occasions.[1] The following
homily takes the form of two questions and answers: *Q.* 'How is
it that Israel is in exile on hostile soil?', *A.* 'She has forsaken
the fount of wisdom'; *Q.* 'Where shall wisdom be found?',
A. 'Wisdom is known to God alone and is none other than the
Law which endureth for ever'. But, before reaching this positive
conclusion, the preacher proceeds, in the manner of Job, to
expound where and how Wisdom is *not* to be found and
to enumerate three types of men who have failed in the
quest.

Now what is the connexion of this discourse on Wisdom with
the 9th of Ab? I find it in the *Haphtarah* for the Fast-day; the
whole section is a sermon on the lesson. The modern Jewish
service still retains the prophetical lesson from Jeremiah (viii. 13–
ix. 24 [23]) for which we have ancient authority,[2] beginning
'I will utterly consume them' and ending 'Let not the wise man
glory', &c. The primitive lesson was doubtless shorter. Two
verses only call for remark, one in the middle (perhaps originally
the opening) of the lesson, the other at the close. In Jer. ix. 12 f.
the same question is asked and the same answer given as in
Baruch. 'Who is the wise man that may understand this? and
(who is) he to whom the mouth of the LORD hath spoken, that he
may declare it? Wherefore is the land perished and burned up
like a wilderness . . .? And the LORD said, Because they have
forsaken my law.' The question 'Who is the wise man?' clearly
had a special appropriateness for the fast, since it recurs at the
close of what is still the alternative lesson for the 9th of Ab
(Hos. xiv. 9): 'Who is wise, and he shall understand these things?
prudent, and he shall know them?'

But the sermon in *Baruch* is yet more closely linked to the
concluding verses of the Jeremiah lesson: 'Let not the wise man
glory in his wisdom, neither let the mighty man glory in his
might, let not the rich man glory in his riches: but let him that
glorieth glory in this, that he understandeth, and knoweth me,

---

[1] Ewald, cited by Kneucker, *ad loc.* This portion of the liturgy was taken
over by the Synagogue from the Temple: Oesterley-Box, *Short Survey of Lit.
of Rabbin. and Med. Judaism,* (1920) 163.

[2] T.B. *Meg.* 31 a (on the authority of Abaye, died 338); Rab, *ibid.,* names
another lesson, Is. i. 21.

that I am the LORD', &c.[1] As I observed, the homilies in the
Pesikta sometimes take for their text the last verse of the lesson.[2]
The same holds good here. The verse 'Let not the wise man
glory', with its three types of the vain-glorious, is the text for
our sermon.

After tracing Israel's pitiful condition to her desertion of the
fount of wisdom, the preacher proceeds in,the central portion of
his homily (vv. 16–28) to give concrete examples of the three
classes named in his text—the πλούσιος, the σοφός, the ἰσχυρός—
who have missed the true wisdom. The classes are marked off
by the thrice repeated refrain: ὁδὸν δὲ ἐπιστήμης οὐκ ἔγνωσαν
(v. 20 of the rulers and the rich), ὁδὸν δὲ σοφίας οὐκ ἔγνωσαν
(v. 23 of the worldly wise), οὐδὲ ὁδὸν ἐπιστήμης ἔδωκεν αὐτοῖς (v. 27
of the strong). The whole should be compared with a strikingly
similar discourse on false and true wisdom in St. Paul's First
Epistle to the Corinthians, reminiscent, I cannot but think, of
sermons to which Saul the Pharisee must often have listened on
the 9th Ab.[3]

First (16–21) the rich, 'they that hoarded up silver and gold,
wherein men trust, and of whose getting there is no end.' With
these he groups the princes of the nations; and here the words
'such as lorded it over the beasts that are on the earth' clearly
allude to Nebuchadnezzar, whose lordship over the beasts of the
field and the fowls of the air is emphasized both in Daniel and in
Jeremiah.[4] The monarch, for whose life prayers were asked in
Part I of our book, is here quoted as an example of the futility
of earthly greatness. The words 'They that had their pastime
with the fowls of the air' seem to be a mockery of the pleasures
of the idle rich.[5] To rulers and rich are added (18) metal-workers
and craftsmen, an intermediate link between the πλούσιοι and
the σοφοί. All these have vanished and gone down to Hades;
a second and a third generation have seen the light but failed
to lay hold on wisdom.

[1] In the LXX this clause has been interpolated into the Song of Hannah, the
New Year's Day *Haphtarah* (1 R. ii. 10); *Rosh Hashanah* and *9 Ab* had penitential features in common.
[2] Wünsche, *Pesikta*, viii; Weber, *Jüd. Theologie auf Grund des Talmud*, (1897)
xxvii.
[3] 1 Cor. i. 18–ii. 16. Cf. Baruch iii. 16 with 1 Cor. ii. 6 ff. (οἱ ἄρχοντες); and (οἱ)
ἐπὶ (τῆς) γῆς Bar. iii. 16, 20, 23, with the repeated ὁ αἰὼν οὗτος and ὁ κόσμος in 1 Cor.
i. 20 f., 27, ii. 6. The preacher's text is quoted in 1 Cor. i. 31.
[4] Dan. ii. 38; Jer. xxvii. 6 (xxxiv. 5 LXX).
[5] Folk-lore tales of Nebuchadnezzar may still be in mind.

At *v.* 22 he passes to the σοφοί: 'it hath not been heard of in Canaan, neither hath it been seen in Teman.' Jeremiah attests the reputation of Teman for wisdom,[1] and our preacher, who draws largely on Job, doubtless has in mind his counsellor Eliphaz the Temanite. With Canaan is linked Arabia: 'the merchants of Merran and [once again] Teman'—probably a corruption of 'Midian and Temah'—the μυθόλογοι (romancers or fable-writers) and other purveyors of earthly wisdom. 'Neither western Phoenicians nor eastern Arabs have found the true wisdom', as Ewald paraphrases. Greek philosophy is ignored; the instances are solely Biblical. This, again, suggests a Syrian (or Palestinian) origin.

As his example of the strong men the preacher selects (26) the mightiest sons of earth, the giants renowned of old (οἱ ὀνομαστοὶ ἀπ' ἀρχῆς, cf. Gen. vi. 4 LXX), who might be expected to have inherited wisdom from their divine progenitors. Yet 'these did not God choose, neither gave he the way of knowledge unto them'.[2] So he sums up the negative side of his sermon: 'there is none that knoweth her way, nor any that comprehendeth her path' (31).

The peroration, with obvious reminiscences, in particular of Job and the Αἴνεσις σοφίας in Ben Sira, possesses a beauty of its own, and contains the famous verse often quoted by the Fathers in proof of the doctrine of the Incarnation. 'Yet *He* hath found her,' I paraphrase, 'He the omniscient, maker of earth and its creatures, the light, the stars', which in a beautiful figure appear as outposts in the celestial army answering *Adsumus* to their names:—

And the stars shined in their stations, and were glad:
He called them, and they said, Here we be:
they shined with gladness unto their Maker.
He is our God, none other shall be accounted of beside Him.
He hath found out every way of knowledge,
and hath given it unto Jacob His servant, And to Israel His
  beloved.

---

[1] Jer. xlix. 7 (xxix. 8 LXX).

[2] It is curious to find an apparent allusion to the giants in a modern prayer for the 9th of Ab, which similarly dilates on the vanity of earthly wisdom. 'What are we? what is our life? ... what is our strength? what is our might? ... Are not all the mighty men as nothing before thee and *the men of name* (אַנְשֵׁי הַשֵּׁם) as though they had never been, and the wise as without wisdom and the understanding as without knowledge?' הקינות לתשעה באב (Polish rite), ed. S. Baer, Rodelheim, 1875, p. 58 f.

Afterward did she [1] appear upon earth, and was conversant
    with men.
This is the book of the commandments of God,
And the law that endureth for ever . . . .

The model is here the Praise of Wisdom in Ecclus. xxiv, and the
sentence 'Afterward did she appear upon earth' *may* be the
preacher's reproduction of Ben Sira's words 'Then the Creator of
all things . . . said, Let thy tabernacle be in Jacob, and thine
inheritance in Israel . . . and so was I established in Sion'.[2]
But the personification of wisdom comes in awkwardly before
the identification with the Book of the Law; [3] the introductory
μετὰ τοῦτο is suspicious; as is also the generalizing 'on earth',
'among men' in a passage characterized by Jewish particularism.
On the whole, therefore, I incline with some hesitation to
Kneucker's view that the verse is a Christian interpolation.

The sermon ends with an appeal to Jacob to turn [4] and lay
hold on Wisdom as discovered in the Law; a warning not to
surrender her glory to 'Another' and her privileges to an alien
nation—alluding, probably, to the rise of Christianity—and a
felicitation upon the race which, with its Temple, has not lost its
claim to be the sole possessors of the knowledge of the will of
God.[5] The Temple is not actually named, but its destruction
seems to be hinted at a little higher up : 'O Israel, how great is,
the house of God! and how large is the place of His possession!'
(iii. 24). 'The house of God', he seems to say, is not the ruined
Temple but the broad universe.

A second link connects this sermon with the 9th of Ab. The
preacher took his text from the *Haphtarah*; but we can also
explain his choice of illustrative literature. That he should
draw on the sapiential books was natural ; but why does he have
recourse to Job in particular and after that to the Αἴνεσις σοφίας
in an apocryphal writing ? Now the studies proper to the 9th
of Ab were strictly limited ; 'the precepts of the Lord which
rejoice the heart' were too exhilarating for the fast-day. We
read in the Talmud : [6] 'The Rabbis taught : "All injunctions
which hold good for mourning hold good also for the 9th Ab.
One must not eat or drink or anoint oneself or put on sandals . . .

---

[1] Or (?) 'He'.

[2] Ecclus. xxiv. 8.

[3] Though there is the same awkwardness in Ecclus.

[4] Recalling another *Haphtarah* for 9 Ab (Hos. xiv. 1).

[5] Cf. Rom. ii. 17.   [6] T. B. *Ta'anith*, 30 a.

One must not read in the Law, the Prophets, or the Writings, nor study Mishnah, Talmud, Midrash, Halachah, or Haggadah. But *one may read and study passages which one is not accustomed to read;*[1] *one may also read from Lamentations, Job, and the threatening passages* (lit. 'the bad words') *in Jeremiah*". R. Jehuda even forbade the reading of unfamiliar passages, placing all books on the Index except Job, Lamentations, and Jeremiah's 'bad words'.[2]

Of the permitted writings Lamentations, of which our book, I suggested, was in a sense a rival, has left no mark on the sermon. On the other hand, its text was drawn from one of the gloomiest of Jeremiads, while Job provided the material for the topic 'Where shall wisdom be found?' The language of Job colours the whole discourse: 'Who hath entered into her treasuries?' (iii. 15); 'Who ... will bring her for choice gold?' (30); 'There is none that knoweth her way, nor any that comprehendeth her path. But He that knoweth all things knoweth her, He found her out with His understanding' (31 ff.); the stars which recall the morning stars singing together (34 f.); the phrase 'saw the light' (20); Teman with the reminiscence of Eliphaz. Again, the Wisdom of Ben Sira, the apocryphal book which came nearest to gaining admission to the canon,[3] would certainly figure among the unfamiliar and, for this occasion, licenced Scriptures.

THE CONSOLATIONS

This brings me to the final or consolatory portion of our book. The National Mission, so to speak, having opened with Repentance and proceeded in quest of Wisdom, closes with Hope. This section falls into seven cantos. The first four begin alike with 'Be of good cheer': θαρσεῖτε λαός μου (iv. 5), θαρρεῖτε τέκνα (iv. 21), θαρρήσατε τέκνα (iv. 27), θάρσει Ἰερουσαλήμ (iv. 30). Most commentators carry subdivision no further. But three more invocations of Jerusalem follow, constituting fresh openings: περίβλεψαι πρὸς ἀνατολάς, Ἰερουσαλήμ (iv. 36), ἔκδυσαι Ἰερουσαλήμ (v. 1), ἀνάστηθι Ἰερουσαλήμ (v. 5). Dr. Swete marks the first two of these, though not the last, by a short break in the

---

[1] אבל קורא הוא במקום שאינו רגיל לקרות (on the principle, apparently, that the unfamiliar must also be uncongenial).

[2] The writer adds that school-children had a holiday (as a penalty!); their ordinary studies would cause unseemly joy.

[3] Ryle, *Canon of O. T.* 184.

text.[1]   These seven subdivisions may be classified again, according to the speaker, in two groups.   The first three cantos, part penitence, part hope, are addressed by mother Zion to her exiled children.   The last four, all Consolation, are God's response, through the seer's mouth, to the bereft mother—promises of retaliation on her foes with glorious visions of a return to Palestine under His leadership.

If I am right in connecting the seven cantos with the seven Consolation sabbaths, the change of speaker and tone after the third canto may be explained.   The three first sabbaths fell in the month of Ab, and in parts of Palestine mourning was kept up until the end of that month.[2]   The four remaining sabbaths fell in the month of Elul, and the 1st of Elul was one of the minor New Years,[3] a foretaste of the greater New Year's day a month later.

That this portion of *Baruch* generally conforms to the sabbath cycle appears from (1) the sevenfold division, (2) the dependence on deutero-Isaiah, which dominates it just as Job dominated the sermon, (3) the coincidence of four of the Isaiah passages which serve as Baruch's model with those read on four of the sabbaths, and (4) the reiterated $\theta \acute{a} \rho \sigma \epsilon \iota$ ($\theta a \rho \sigma \epsilon \hat{\iota} \tau \epsilon$) which seems deliberately intended to recall the name by which the sabbaths were known.[4] The Consolation *Haphtaroth*, writes Dr. Büchler, ' formed the texts for homilies containing words of hope and encouragement '.[5] The *Baruch* Consolations are, in my belief, such short poetical homilies, designed to be read or sung on the respective sabbaths as an accompaniment to the Lessons.   If this theory is sound, we have in *Baruch*, the earliest witness, apart from the scene in the synagogue at Nazareth,[6] to the lectionary use of the Book of Isaiah.   In Dr. Büchler's opinion, the employment of lessons from Isaiah first came into vogue on these particular sabbaths.[7]

---

[1] It is just possible that the three final cantos are a later appendix to bring up the total to seven.   They lack the initial word of good cheer ; they run parallel to the eleventh of the Psalms of Solomon ; while no. (5) is practically a duplicate of the first part of no. (7).   Anyhow the transmitted text is clearly divisible into seven sections.

[2] Sepphoris and Tiberias are mentioned ; T. J. *Ta'anith* (tr. Schwab, Gemara following iv. 6).

[3] For tithes of cattle ; T. B. *Rosh Hash.* i. 1.

[4] דנחמתא *consolationis.*

[5] *J. Q. R.* vi. 72.

[6] Luke iv. 17.

[7] Although he would bring the date down to as late as A. D. 200.

MONTH	Sabbath	Is.	H(APHTARAH)	Bar.	C(ANTO)	PSALM OF SOLOMON xi.
AB	(I)	xl. 1-9	'COMFORT YE MY PEOPLE' ZION'S TIDINGS TO THE CITIES OF JUDAH	iv. 5-9 / 12, 19	θαρσεῖτε λαός μου ZION'S TIDINGS TO αἱ πάροικοι σειών / THE DESERTED WIDOW (cf. H. II)	
	(II)	xlix. 14 / 18 / 21	ZION'S COMPLAINT OF GOD'S FORGETFULNESS VISION OF GATHERING CHILDREN (1) THE DESERTED WIDOW (LXX)	21	[Exhortation to patience and promise of speedy delivery]	
	(III)	liv. 11	['O thou afflicted ... and not comforted']	27-	'YE SHALL BE REMEMBERED OF HIM' (cf. H. II)	
ELUL	(IV)	li. 12- / 17-	'I (even) I AM YOUR COMFORTER' FURY AND DOOM OF OPPRESSOR REPRISALS—THE CUP OF πτῶσις	30-	'HE THAT NAMED THEE WILL COMFORT THEE', DOOM OF THE OPPRESSOR REPRISALS IN KIND—πτῶσις	
	(V)	liv. 1-	['Sing, o barren ....']	36-	VISION OF GATHERING CHILDREN (1)	3- V. OF GATHERING CHILDREN
	(VI)	lx. 1-	['Arise, shine ...'] ZION'S λαμπρότης DRAWS THE NATIONS VISION OF GATHERING CHILDREN (2): DAUGHTERS CARRIED ON SHOULDERS (LXX)	v. 1-	ZION'S INVESTITURE (cf. H. VII) ZION'S λαμπρότης SHOWN TO THE WORLD HER NEW NAMES (cf. H. VII)	5- Subservient Nature (cf. C. VII)
	(VII) {	lxi. 10- / lxii. 2(-)	['I will greatly rejoice ...'] ZION'S INVESTITURE HER NEW NAME(S)	5-	V. OF GATHERING CHILDREN (2): CARRIED AS (ON) A ROYAL THRONE (cf. H. VI) Subservient Nature	8 ZION'S INVESTITURE

¹ The prophet's order is here abandoned; chap. li follows liv, as if this lesson had been designedly allocated to the fourth sabbath, the first after the month of mourning.

The parallel between *Haphtaroth* and cantos is not absolutely precise. Exact correspondence in *position* is confined to Cantos (1) and (4) which are based respectively on the lessons for the first and fourth of the sabbaths. In other instances the same passages of Isaiah are employed, but not in the order in which they stand in the *Pesikta*. Since, however, traditions vary as to the *Haphtaroth* and their order, and our book must represent a very early arrangement, this difference presents no serious difficulty.

The relation between the Isaiah lessons which, according to the most widely attested arrangement,[1] were read on the seven sabbaths and the Baruch cantos will appear from the Table, p. 102. Upright capitals indicate correspondence between *Haphtarah* and Canto in both subject and position; sloping capitals correspondence in subject but not in position.

The antiquity of this cycle of lessons is beyond doubt, though its origin and development are obscure. Doubtless it grew from smaller beginnings.[2] I need not repeat Dr. Büchler's theory as to its growth; but it is noteworthy that he regards as the oldest of the lessons the first and the fourth, which provide the model for the first and the fourth cantos.[3] A third ancient *Haphtarah* was probably the last (ZION'S INVESTITURE), which sets the tone for the penultimate Canto.

These three passages, moreover, illustrate the two principles which appear to have governed the selection. Those principles were that either the word 'comfort' must actually occur, as it does in (I) and (IV), or the first word must be duplicated, as it is in all three instances: 'Comfort ye, comfort ye', 'I (even) I', 'Exulting I will exult'. The Jews (with some modern authorities) interpreted the words in the first *Haphtarah* 'She hath received of the LORD's hand *double* for all her sins'[4] to mean 'double *compensation* for all her penalties', and fancifully saw a symbol of this in the duplicated words. Another system arranges the lessons on this principle, for six Consolation sabbaths only, i. e. double the number of *Straf-sabbate*, and each lesson beginning with a double word.[5] The former principle, the occurrence of

---

[1] Found in the older *Pesikta*, the later *Pesikta Rabbathi*, and the *Tosafoth Megillah*.

[2] Maimonides knew of only one consolation passage as the ancient custom (*J. Q. R.* vi. 64).

[3] *J. Q. R. loc. cit.* [4] Is. xl. 2.

[5] So the Midrash Tanchuma (on Deut. i). The list is xl. 1, li. 12, li. 9, li. 17, lxi. 10, xxxv. 2.

the word 'comfort', which gave its name to the series, is doubt-less the older of the two.[1]

I can but glance at the outstanding parallels between cantos and lessons.

Canto 1 (iv. 5–20). Mother Zion's first address to her children is prefaced by a divine consolation through the seer's mouth. The topic—the reason for Israel's evil plight—links this canto to the sermon for the fast-day.

The opening words Θαρσεῖτε λαός μου are an unmistakable echo of the first *Haphtarah* נחמו נחמו עמי. In Isaiah, of course, the verb is transitive, and 'my people' is object (not vocative); the prophets (or, as in the LXX, the priests) are commissioned to console God's people. But this is just what the prophet is here doing; nor, even if he did render his model ' Be comforted O my people', would he stand alone.[2]

In *v.* 9 Zion takes up the λόγος παρακλήσεως and remains the speaker until the end of the third canto. In her first words we have a second reminiscence of the *Haphtarah*. Before turning to her own children she addresses her πάροικοι (fem.), not, as in the R.V., ' ye *women* that dwell about Zion', but the neighbour *cities*, which are mentioned twice again (*vv.* 14, 24). They have witnessed the calamity of the Holy City, and are warned not to exult over the deserted widow, but to reflect on the cause of her woes; they will (the next canto tells them) speedily behold her deliverance. In this address to the πάροικοι we have surely an echo of the prophet's call to Jerusalem to announce to her ' daughter-cities' (Cheyne) the near approach of God : ' Say unto *the cities of Judah*, Behold your God ' (Is. xl. 9).

This canto affords no more parallels to the first *Haphtarah*, but the thought which pervades it of the desolate and bereft widow comes from the second,[3] as if two lessons had been run together. At the close she turns to her children whom she is powerless to help. With resignation she witnesses their departure after the fateful 9th Ab. She exchanges the garment of peace for the sackcloth of prayer, and will continue to cry unto the Everlasting ἐν ταῖς ἡμέραις μου. 'As long as I live' is the usual rendering;

---

[1] In *Baruch* the double word is not found (even θαρσεῖτε iv. 5 is not dupli-cated), except in the last instance where the Syriac supplies it ('Arise, arise').

[2] Cf. Vulg. ' consolamini, consolamini, popule meus'.

[3] Cf. 12 τῇ χήρᾳ καὶ καταλειφθείσῃ, 16 τῆς χήρας, 19 ἐγὼ γὰρ κατελείφθην ἔρημος with Is. xlix. 21 LXX ἐγὼ δὲ ἄτεκνος καὶ χήρα . . . ἐγὼ δὲ κατελείφθην μόνη.

but may we not see an allusion to the 'days of season' for which the book is designed?

Cantos 2 and 3, in which the Mother bids her children follow her example of penitent prayer, offer no verbal parallels to the corresponding lessons.[1] One leading idea of the second *Haphtarah* has however, as we saw, been anticipated, and another, that of God's forgetfulness, colours both these cantos.[2]

At *Canto 4* (iv. 30-35) there is a new Speaker. The Mother city now becomes the recipient of divine consolation. The month of mourning is over and New Year draws on. No more mention of chastisement and the Chastiser (ὁ ἐπαγαγών); consolation fills the field. Exordium and contents alike link this fourth canto to the Lesson for the fourth sabbath. Θάρσει, 'Ιερουσαλήμ, παρακαλέσει σε ὁ ὀνομάσας σε opens the canto. 'I, even I, am he that comforteth you' begins the Lesson.[3] Reprisals form the topic of both. Isaiah dwells on the futility of 'the fury of the oppressor' and the transfer into his hand of 'the cup of staggering'. Baruch, with a particular enemy in view, voicing the national thirst for vengeance of the generation following the year 70, enlarges on the oppressor's doom. 'Woe to them that afflicted thee, and rejoiced at thy fall! Woe to the cities to which thy children became bond-servants! Woe to the city that received[4] thy sons!' As she rejoiced at Zion's fall, so shall she mourn for her own desolation. In revenge for the burnt Temple (so we may read between the lines) she will burn 'for many days' with heaven-sent fire, and thereafter become the abode of devils.[5] One little verbal parallel may be added. The two words used in this canto of Zion's fall, πτῶμα and πτῶσις, occur in the LXX of deutero-Isaiah only in the corresponding *Haphtarah*.

Cantos 5-7 (iv. 36-v. 9). The three final cantos may be considered together. That the Consolation Lessons still form the background is evident from the reappearance in *Baruch* of the themes of two of them, though in a different order; it is known

---

[1] The nearest parallel to the third short canto is Is. lv. 6 f. which in the modern service is used on all fast days.

[2] The speaker in Lesson (2), as in canto (2), is Zion herself: '*But Zion said*, The LORD hath forgotten me' (Is. xlix. 14). The exhortation to long suffering in the second canto (μακροθυμήσατε 25) and the promised remembrance in the third (27) are apparently the answer to the complaint of forgetfulness.

[3] Is. li. 12. 'Thy namer', a substitute for 'Thy maker' (Is. li. 13), seems to come from the Lesson for the seventh sabbath (*ib.* lxii. 2).

[4] Perhaps corrupt.

[5] Cf. Jer. ix. 11 (the *Haphtarah* for 9th Ab).

that the order of the three last *Haphtaroth* was variable.[1] But in
two respects these cantos stand apart from the rest. The introductory θάρσει is absent. Beside the Isaiah lessons a third
document, running parallel to these verses, has to be considered,
viz. the eleventh of the Psalms of Solomon.

The relation between the three documents is shown in the
Table above (p. 102). The following results emerge. (i) The themes
of *Haphtaroth* (6) and (7) recur in *Baruch*, though in different order.
(ii) *Baruch* has no counterpart to *Haphtarah* (5). But this
Haphtarah is likewise unrepresented in the later *Pesikta Rabbathi*, where it is replaced by two passages from Zechariah.
(iii) In *Baruch* its place is taken by the duplicated Vision of the
GATHERING CHILDREN. (iv) In both *Baruch* and the Psalm
an additional theme appears, which I call SUBSERVIENT
NATURE ; a picture based partly on Isaiah xl, partly on Jewish
Midrash, of mountains and hills brought low, valleys filled to
make a level road, and trees crowding into a shade, at the
bidding of God who leads the returning host. It looks as if
a scheme originally designed for six sabbaths has been amplified
in various ways to make up the round number seven.

A word as to the little Psalm of Solomon. It begins ' Blow ye
the trumpet in Sion, the holy trumpet of Jubilee '.[2] The
' trumpet of Jubilee' is significant, as it links the Psalm to the
Feast of Trumpets or New Year, and the sabbaths we have now
reached immediately preceded the New Year. It ends with
a short prayer, and in the centre gives a little picture of the
exiles' return with the three themes shown in the Table. Bishop
Ryle and Dr. James have adduced strong, I think convincing,
arguments for the dependence of Baruch on the Psalm. The
parallels in the added theme, SUBSERVIENT NATURE, are
specially striking. It will be observed, however, that in these
cantos Baruch has parallels with the Lessons which are absent
from the Psalm ; it cannot be urged that he knows the Isaiah
passages only through the medium of the Psalm. The themes are
moreover rearranged, and the three cantos are only part of a
larger whole, all dependent on deutero-Isaiah. It is therefore
conceivable that the affinity between Baruch and Solomon is due
to mutual dependence on some older document. It seems probable, however, that Baruch has in this portion, beside the
Consolation *Haphtaroth*, made free use of the Greek Psalm of

---

[1] *J. Q. R.* vi. 70.

[2] ἐν σάλπιγγι σημασίας ἁγίων (tr. Ryle and James).

Solomon as a subsidiary source.   Whether the Psalm itself has any connexion with an earlier stage in the sabbath cycle must be left an open question.

That the concluding section of *Baruch* is based upon the cycle is, I venture to think, beyond doubt.   The sevenfold arrangement and the recurrence in the canto of the theme of the lesson in four (or five) instances out of seven can hardly be fortuitous.

External evidence of liturgical use.

From the internal evidence as to the designed liturgical use of the book I turn to the meagre and uncertain external evidence for its actual use in Jewish worship.   The author's design, as I said, may never have been realized in its entirety; yet the evidence, so far as it goes, curiously fits in with the results already obtained.

I begin with the negative evidence of Jerome, who states that the Hebrews neither read nor even possessed the book: 'librum autem Baruch . . . qui *apud Hebraeos nec legitur nec habetur* praetermisimus.' [1]   But Jerome's interests were confined to Palestinian practice and did not extend to the Dispersion.

Against his remark we have to set two positive statements. Both emanate from the region of Upper Syria.   One dates from the fourth century ; the other is ostensibly of the same date, but may be a century or so later.   The occasions indicated for the reading of Baruch differ in our two authorities ; one of them is ambiguous.

(1) *Evidence of the Apostolical Constitutions.*   The first passage occurs in the *Apostolical Constitutions* (v. 20), a work compiled, as is now generally admitted, in the latter part of the fourth century by the interpolator of the Epistles of St. Ignatius.   In an enumeration of Christian festivals the writer, after mentioning the Feast of the Ascension, alludes to the future coming of Christ, when the Jews shall look upon the Beloved of God whom they pierced and recognizing Him shall mourn for themselves.   He proceeds : ' For even now, *on the tenth day of the month Gorpiaeus,*[2] they assemble and read the Lamentations of Jeremiah in which it is said . . . [here he quotes Lam. iv. 20 LXX] . . . *and Baruch*

---

[1] In the prologue to his translation of Jeremiah.   Cf. the prologue to his commentary ' nec habetur apud Hebraeos '.

[2] Two inferior MSS. insert λῴου before γορπιαίου.   There is stronger authority for prefixing ἐννάτου: ' on the tenth of the ninth month Gorpiaeus.'   See Funk's edition (1905).

in which is written "This is our God... [here he quotes the last
verses of Bar. iii ending with the familiar words].... Afterward did He appear upon earth and was conversant with men".
And', he continues, ' when they read, they bewail and lament, as
they suppose for the desolation wrought by Nebuchadnezzar, but
in reality they unwillingly rehearse (προοίμια ποιοῦνται ἄκοντες)
the mourning which will hereafter befall them.'

The *Constitutions* is a compilation of older works. Its main
source at this point is the *Didascalia Apostolorum*, written a century earlier; but this whole section is much expanded in the
Constitutions. In the *Didascalia* the parallel passage runs: ' As
also, after the mourning of the Christ,[1] even until now, *on the ninth
of the month Ab*, they read in the Lamentations of Jeremiah and
assemble and wail and lament ...'

Thus the earlier *Didascalia* names Lamentations only, not
Baruch, and as the date of the Jews' mourning the 9th of Ab;
the later work mentions Baruch as well, and for date the 10th of
Gorpiaeus.

Two questions arise. (1) May we equate the two dates mentioned, the 9th Ab (*Did.*) and the 10th Gorpiaeus (*Const.*)? (2)
Had the author of the *Constitutions* warrant for his additional information as to the reading of Baruch?

The Syrian writer of the *Constitutions* employs the Syro-Mace-
donian calendar, and we are left to discover the Jewish equivalent
for the month named. Most commentators identify the 10th
Gorpiaeus in this passage with the 10th of Tishri, the Day of
Atonement. If we may trust the reckoning followed by Josephus
and others, the equation should run :—

Syro-Macedonian	Hebrew	English		
(10) Lous	= Ab	= approximately July		
(11) Gorpiaeus	= Elul	=	,,	August
(12) Hyperberetaeus	= Tishri	=	,,	September

Gorpiaeus, in this system, coincides neither with Ab nor with
Tishri, but with the intervening month of Elul, which can hardly
be intended. The choice lies between the 10th Tishri and the
9th (or 10th) Ab. I think we are justified in deciding for the
latter date, because Lamentations, which is named along with

---

[1] Or (?) ' for the Messiah '.

Baruch, has always been read on the 9th Ab, and I know of no evidence for its use on the Day of Atonement. That the writer mentions the tenth, not the ninth, is intelligible, because Josephus,[1] with some Rabbinical authorities, dated the double burning of the Temple on the 10th Ab, although in Palestine it was always commemorated on the ninth.

I am, however, bound to admit that expert authorities are sceptical as to the value of any information which the author of the *Constitutions* did not derive from his sources, and incline to regard it as his own invention and not based on tradition. Professor C. H. Turner, in a private communication, writes that he 'should hesitate to use this reference as any indication of actual Jewish usage'. He would regard 'the existence of the well-known passage in Baruch, referred by early Christians to the Incarnation', as 'the sole ultimate reason for the naming of Baruch side by side with Lamentations'. On the other hand, it may be urged that the passage quoted occurs in the Homily on Wisdom, which on internal grounds we found reason for connecting with the 9th Ab. The external evidence, if I have correctly interpreted it, confirms this. Again, if the statement in the *Constitutions* stood alone, we might perhaps dismiss it as untrustworthy. But we have another witness from the same region to the use of *Baruch* in Jewish worship.

(2) *Evidence of a work ascribed to Ephraim Syrus.* In this case *Baruch* is not named, but a quotation is made from it which the Jewish synagogue are represented as singing on a date shortly before Passover. The passage occurs in a Palm Sunday sermon or diatribe against the Jews entitled 'A sermon against the Jews delivered on the first of the week of Hosannas, of the same our father, the holy Mar Ephraim the Syrian'.[2] The ascription to St. Ephraim is, Professor Burkitt tells me, probably incorrect; the Homily appears to be later than A.D. 498, at about which date, as we are told by a contemporary writer,[3] Palm Sunday was first observed as a festival at Edessa. Whatever its date, the sermon is remarkable, not only for the light thrown on the early observance of Palm Sunday (regarded as the Feast of Christ *par excellence*), but also for its allusion to a fast held simultaneously by

[1] *B. I.* vi. 250 (iv. 5).

[2] Syriac-Latin ed. of St. Ephraim's works, Rome 1743, iii. 209 ff.; Engl. trans. by J. B. Morris, *Select works of St. Ephrem* in the Oxford *Library of the Fathers*, 1847, 61 ff. I quote from the latter.

[3] Joshua Stylites, cap. xxxii.

the Jews.[1]   And, though this fast occurs at the spring New Year, it is noteworthy that the special allusions are to the destruction of Jerusalem, and to events commonly associated with the 9th Ab and the other 'national calamity' fast-days.

After extolling the Christian festival the preacher turns (§ 8) to the Jews.   'He cut off the crowns to-day, loosening the crown of Judah; and the Lord caused the ruler to pass from his people. ... To-day the congregation that loved feast-days sitteth in sorrow; because she declined the feast-day of the Son, He hath despised and rejected her feast-days.[2]   To-day the glory passed away from the people of Israel . . . To-day the breaches are multiplied in the dwellings of Jacob. . : .'   Then comes the Baruch quotation.   ' *To-day let the synagogue sing this song among the people :* " *He hath brought upon me a great mourning :* the Lord *hath left me desolate,* and the Lord hath forgotten[3] that I am his heritage, and hath reckoned me as a stranger, and *as a widow that is bereaved* ".'   Here we have a clear reference to the first of the Baruch cantos : ' God hath brought upon me a great mourning . . . the widow bereft of many . . . I am left desolate.'[4]   Later on the preacher reverts to the Jews and asks (§ 15), like the preacher in *Baruch,* 'What is thine iniquity, O daughter of Jacob, that thy chastisement is so severe?' and returns a similar answer.   Yet for all this, he proceeds (§ 16), the nation 'now thinks within itself that a restoration shall be again given unto it . . . Lo! it expecteth and searches into the times when its release shall be.   It reads foolishly in the Prophets and understandeth not their words . . . With blustering voice it cries that Jerusalem shall be built again . . .'; and then, quoting the consolation passages from Isaiah on which *Baruch* draws, the Saint rounds upon his adversaries (§ 20) : 'Learn, therefore, O Hebrew, that the Lord *hath* built Jerusalem, and raised up her walls firm, and blessed her children with peace.'

This sermon was delivered on Palm Sunday.   We learn from it that in the sixth century, if not earlier, the first of the Baruch cantos was chanted in the Jewish synagogue at or in the neighbourhood of Edessa on that day.   The context suggests that

---

[1] The appropriation of Jewish prophecies to Christian use is another interesting feature ; while behind both Jewish and Christian ritual we may trace the influence of a pagan festival in honour of the spring.

[2] Cf. Lam. i. 1, ii. 6 (LXX).

[3] Cf. Is. xlix. 14 (the *Haphtarah* for the second sabbath after 9 Ab).

[4] Bar. iv. 9, 12, 19.

a larger use of the book may have been made. Now the Jewish reckoning of Easter continued in Syria after its proscription by the Council of Nicaea.[1] Palm Sunday, according to this reckoning, would approximately coincide with the 10th of Nisan. Thus, if we were right in regarding the date in Bar. i. 8 as a misplaced gloss on *v.* 14, the Syriac reading in that verse ' on the 10th of Nisan' finds a remarkable confirmation in this Syriac homily. The homily further supports the conjecture that the ' feast' on which ' Baruch' or the Jewish Dispersion which he represented desired his book to be read was that of the spring New Year. Why the mourning ceremony should fall in the spring is not clear. I can only conjecture that the Jews of northern Syria, following old Babylonian custom, kept their New Year feast in the spring, and in connexion with it a Day of Atonement on the 10th Nisan, answering to the Palestinian fast of the 10th Tishri at the autumn New Year.

In an unworked field provisional results only can be expected. I hope that these concluding lectures may at least have convinced my readers that ' the liturgical factor in Biblical interpretation' is one which we cannot afford to neglect. One thought remains. British arms have in these latter days been privileged to bring some of the dreams of the ancient Zionists within reach of realization. It may be hoped that British statesmanship may be enabled to complete the difficult task and to satisfy those aspirations, without the bloodshed which the Jews of old regarded as the necessary preliminary to their fulfilment. Their debtors we are ; and, as part of our rich spiritual heritage from Judaism, the Book of Baruch has its lesson for us, in pointing to the path of penitence, leading on to the quest for wisdom to reconstruct our national life, as the road to our goal and ultimately, may be, to consolation for our years of trial.

[1] Professor Burkitt tells me that Aphraates (*De Paschate*, Demonstr. xii) 'fixes the Christian celebration of the Passion by the Jewish Passover'. His rule appears to be : ' Let Easter Sunday be always the Sunday next after 14 Nisan.'

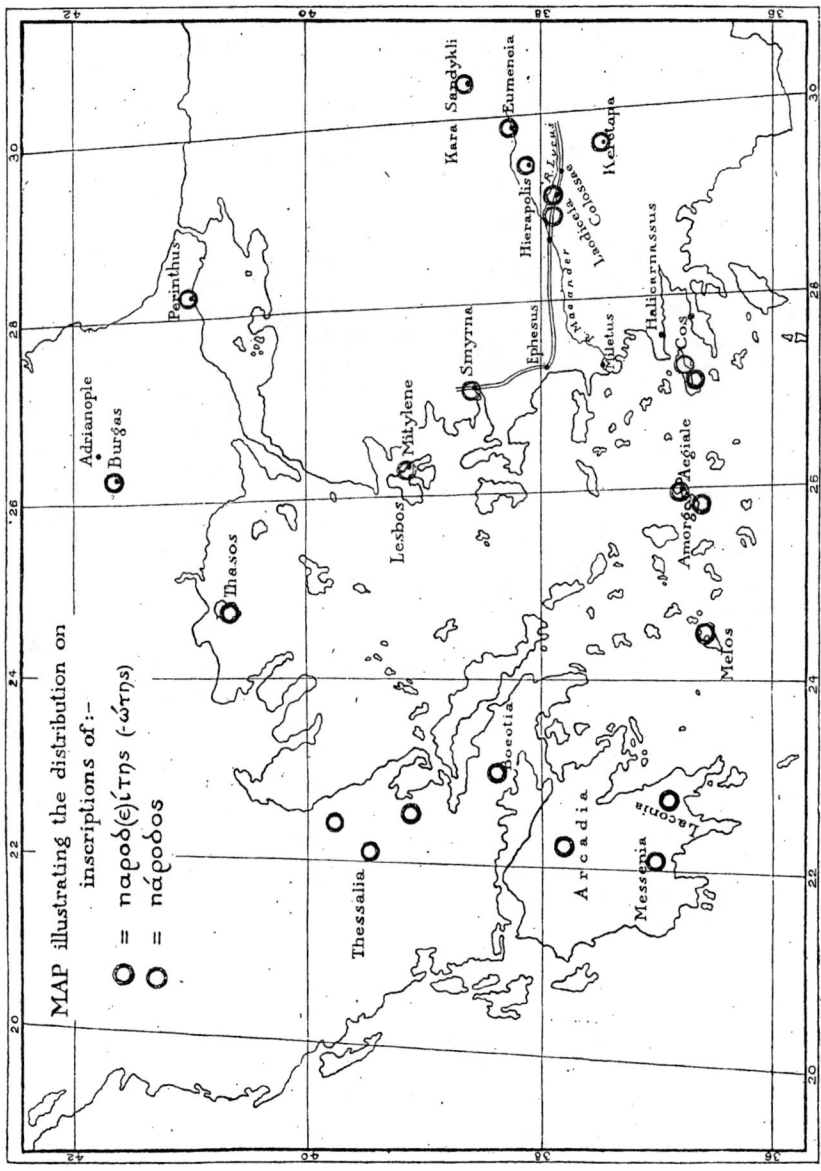

MAP illustrating the distribution on inscriptions of :-

○ = παροδ(ε)ίτης (ώτης)

○ = πάροδος

Adrianople
○ Burgas

Perinthus

Thasos

Lesbos
Mitylene

Smyrna

Kara Sapdykli

Eumeneia

Hierapolis

R. Lycus

Keramal

Laodicea Colossae

Maeander

Ephesus

Miletus

Halicarnassus

Cos

Amorgos Aegiale

Melos

Thessalia

Boeotia

Arcadia

Messenia

Laconia

APPENDICES

APPENDIX I

THE BOOKS OF REIGNS: TABLE SHOWING CHARACTERISTICS OF THE LATER TRANSLATOR

THE text used for this and subsequent Tables is, unless otherwise stated, that of cod. B. The late portions are those entitled βγ and γδ (collectively βδ).

	Hebrew		α = 1 Regn.	ββ = 2 R. i. 1-xi. 1	βγ = 2 R. xi. 2-R. ii. 11	γγ = 3 R. ii. 12-xxi. 43	γδ = 3 R. xxii, 4 R.
		ADJECTIVES AND SUBSTANTIVES					
(1)	גדול (איש)	ἁδρύς	—	—	2 R. xv. 18 B, 3 R. i. 9 B	—	4 R. x. 6, 11
(2)	שופר	κερατίνη	—	—	2 R. xv. 10, xviii. 16, xx. 1, 22 3 R. i. 34, 39, 41	—	4 R. ix, 13
		Contrast σάλπιγξ	xiii. 3	ii. 28, vi. 15	—	—	—¹
(3)	גדוד	μονόζωνος	—	—	2 R. xxii. 30	—	4 R. v. 2, vi. 23, xiii. 20 f., xxiv. 2 quater
		Contrast γεδδούρ	xxx. 8, 15 bis, 23	—	—	—	—
		ἐξοδία	—	iii. 22	—	—	—
		σύστρεμμα	—	iv. 2	—	xi. 14	—
		CONJUNCTIONS, PARTICLES, ETC.					
(4)	Misc.	ἀνθ' ὧν ὅτι Cf.	—	—	2 R. xii. 6, 10	—	4 R. xviii. 12 B, xxii. 19
	יען אשר	ἀνθ' ὧν ὅσα	—	—	—	—	4 R. x. 30, xxi. 11, 15
(5)	מעל	ἀπάνωθεν Cf.	—	—	2 R. xi. 20, 24, xx. 21 3 R. i. 53	—	4 R. ii. 3 B*, 5 A
		ἐπάνωθεν	—	—	2 R. xi. 21, xiii. 9, xxiv. 25 3 R. ii. 4	—²	10 times in 4 R. (including var. lect. in ii. 3, 5)

¹ σάλπιγξ renders another Hebrew word in this book.
² ἐπάνωθεν renders other Hebrew words in 3 R. vii f.

	Hebrew		α = 1 Regn.	ββ = 2 R. i.1- xi. 1	βγ = 2 R. xi. 2- 3 R. ii. 11	γγ = 3 R. ii. 12-xxi. 43	γδ = 3 R. xxii, 4 R.
		CONJUNCTIONS, PARTICLES, ETC. (*continued*)					
(6)	Misc.	ἡνίκα	—[1]	—	2 R. xii. 21, xiii. 36, xvi. 16, xvii. 27, xx. 13	—	4 R. iv. 18, xvii. 31
(7)	גם	καί γε	—[2]	ii. 6 A, 7 BA[2] (= וגם)	29 times in B, 24 in A 2 R. xi. 12- xxi. 20 3 R. i. 6, 48, ii. 5	—[2]	17 times in B, 15 in A 3 R. xxii. 22 4 R. ii. 5, &c.
(8)	אבל	καὶ μάλα[3]	—	—	2 R. xiv. 5, 3 R. i. 43	—	4 R. iv. 14
		SYNTAX					
(9)	אנכי	ἐγώ εἰμι with finite verb	—	—[4]	2 R. xi. 5, xii. 7, xv. 28, xviii. 12, xx. 17, xxiv. 12, 17 3 R. ii. 2	—[5]	4 R. iv. 13, x. 9, xxii. 20
(10)		Historic present	151 exx.	28 exx.	2 R. xi. 7, xiv. 27 *bis*, 30, xvii. 17 *bis.*[6]	48 exx.	4 R. i. 18 a [vii. 5, 10][6]

[1] ἡνίκα occurs in 1 R. i. 24 A (B omits clause).

[2] καί γε appears in Hexaplaric interpolations in the A text in 1 R. xviii. 5, xix. 20, 24 ; 2 R. iii. 19 ; 3 R. vii. 17.

[3] Elsewhere thus only in Dan. (LXX) x. 21.

[4] σὺ εἶ . . . ἐλάλησας 2 R. vii. 29 B is not parallel ; εἶ has come from the previous verse.

[5] Contrast ἐγώ ii. 16, 18, 20, &c.

[6] For these doubtful instances see p. 20.

APPENDIX II

THE TRANSLATORS OF JEREMIAH: TABLE OF RENDERINGS

THE figures in brackets after a Greek word indicate the number of times it is used.

	Hebrew	Jeremiah α (i–xxix. 7)[1]	Jeremiah β (xxix. 8[1]–li)
1	כה אמר יהוה	τάδε λέγει Κύριος (about 60 times) down to xxix. 1, 8 [13 AQ]	οὕτως εἶπεν Κύριος (about 70 times) xxx. 1–li. 34
			τάδε εἶπεν[2] Κύριος xxix. 13 Bℵ
2	יצת hiph. 'kindle'	ἀνάψω πῦρ καὶ καταφάγεται xvii. 27, xxi. 14 (καὶ ἔδεται), xxvii. 32	καύσω πῦρ καὶ καταφ. xxx. 16
3	שמה (שממה) 'desolation'	ἀφανισμός (18) ix. 11–xxviii. 62	ἄβατος (-ον)[3] (13) xxix. 14–li. 22
4	לקח מוסר	δέξασθαι παιδείαν ii. 30, v. 3, vii. 28, xvii. 23	λαβεῖν παιδείαν xxxix. 33, xlii. 13
5	רפא	ἰᾶσθαι (7)	ἰατρεύειν (4) [Also xxviii. 9 ἰατρεύσαμεν . . . καὶ οὐκ ἰάθη]
6	הנני מביא	ἰδοὺ ἐγὼ ἐπάγω v. 15, vi. 19, xi. 11, xix. 3, 15 [li. 35]	ἰδοὺ ἐγὼ φέρω xxx. 5, xlii. 17, xlvi. 16
			ἰδοὺ ἐγὼ ἄγω xxxviii. 8
7	עת	καιρός (27) ii. 27–xxviii. 18	χρόνος xxix. 9, xxxvii. 7, xxxviii. 1
8	שכן	κατασκηνοῦν vii. 12, xvii. 6, xxiii. 6, xxviii. 13	καταλύειν xxix. 17, xxx. 9, xxxii. 10
9	נחם niph. (of *Divine* repentance)	μετανοεῖν iv. 28, xviii. 8, 10[4]	παύεσθαι xxxiii. 3, 13, 19[5]
			ἀναπαύεσθαι xlix. 10

[1] The exact point of transition from α to β is uncertain; a mixture of the two styles occurs at the juncture.

[2] A unique instance of this mixture. Of the converse mixture, οὕτως λέγει, I have noted four instances in the B text, two in either part: xiv. 10, xxiii. 16; xli. 4, xlii. 13.

[3] In α ἄβατος occurs four times, as an adj. with γῆ or ἔρημος. In β, in the phrase εἶναι εἰς ἄβατον, it becomes almost an abstract noun; cf. the vb. ἀβατοῦν xxix. 21.

[4] Jer. β uses μεταν. only of human repentance (xxxviii. 19).

[5] xxxviii. 15 B* = 'be comforted' (παρακληθῆναι cett.).

	Hebrew	Jeremiah a (i–xxix. 7)	Jeremiah β (xxix. 8–li)
10	נוה	νομή x. 25, xxiii. 3, xxvii. 7, 19, 45 [Also = other Hebrew words]	τόπος xxix. 20, xxxii. 16 κατάλυσις xxix. 21 κατάλυμα xl. 12
11	נגב	νότος xiii. 19 (πόλ. αἱ πρὸς νότ.), xvii. 26	νάγεβ xxxix. 44 = xl. 13 (ἐν πόλεσιν τῆς ν.)
12	כעם hiph.	παροργίζειν vii. 18 f., viii. 19, xi. 17, xxv. 6	πικραίνειν xxxix. 32 B, xl. 9, xliv. 15 παραπικραίνειν xxxix. 29, 32 אA
13	'his soul shall be for a prey' (שלל)	ἔσται ἡ ψυχὴ αὐτοῦ εἰς σκῦλα xxi. 9 (cf. εἰς προνομήν xxvii. 10)	ἔσται ἡ ψ. (αὐτοῦ) εἰς εὕρεμα xlv. 2, xlvi. 18, cf. li. 35
14	שדד	ταλαιπωρεῖν iv. 13 (οὐαὶ ἡμῖν ὅτι ταλαιπωροῦμεν), 20 bis, ix. 19, x. 20 (with doublet ὤλετο), xii. 12 (xxviii. 48 Q^mg) ταλαιπωρία (iv. 20 = al.) vi. 7, 26 (ἥξει ταλ.), xv. 8, xx. 8, xxviii. 35, 56	ὄλλυσθαι[1] xxix. 11, xxx. 3, xxxi. 1 (οὐαὶ ἐπὶ N. ὅτι ὤλετο), 15, 18, 20, xxxviii. 2 ὄλεθρος xxxi. 3, 8 (ἥξει ὄλ.), 32
	שר, שדד		
15	שמחה) ששון)	χαρά xv. 16, xvi. 9, xxv. 10	χαρμοσύνη (χαρμονή) xxxi. 33 (-μονή א^{c.a} Q), xxxviii. 13 Q (-μονή Bא), xl. 11 (-μονή A)

Among other words characteristic of Jer. a, and absent from the β portion, may be noted ἀσεβεῖν and ἀσέβεια, διασκορπίζειν, διαφθείρειν and διαφθορά, δοκιμάζειν and δοκιμαστός, ἐκδικεῖν and ἐκδίκησις, κακία—κακοποιεῖν—κάκωσις, καταδυναστεύειν, κληρονομία, σόφος, τάσσειν (e. g. τὴν γῆν εἰς ἔρημον), ὑπάρχειν, ὡσεί.

Of β words attention may be called to ἀποκλαίεσθαι, ἀποστολή (xxxix. 36, cf. Bar. ii. 25; Heb. דֶּבֶר 'pestilence', rendered by θάνατος in Jer. a and xli. 17), ἀποτρέχειν, βομβεῖν (cf. βόμβησις Bar. ii. 29), γένος, δύναμις (25 times; in a 4 times), δυνατός, ἐνοικεῖν, ἐπίχειρον = 'arm' (xxxi. 25, xxxiv. 4; cf. 2 Macc. xv. 33, Vulg. manum; in classical Greek only in the plural = 'wages'), ἡγεμών (= שר), καθά, πολίτης ('fellow-citizen' = רע, xxxvi. 23, xxxviii. 34; so only elsewhere in Prov.), πρὸς τό (μή) with inf., συντάσσειν, φόβος, χρηματίζειν, ψευδοπροφήτης (= נביא; once in a, vi. 13). The anarthrous infinitive is common in β; rare in a.

The vocabulary of Jer. a, as a rule, finds illustration in Ezekiel a and the Minor Prophets.

---

[1] The simplex ὀλλύναι is confined elsewhere in LXX to Proverbs and Job.

APPENDIX III

THE TRANSLATORS OF EZEKIEL: TABLES OF RENDERINGS

The phenomena are a little more complicated than in Jeremiah. The various strata are as follows:—

Ez. α embracing $\left\{ \begin{array}{l} \text{Ez. } \alpha \text{ (i)} = \text{i–xxvii.} \\ \text{Ez. } \alpha \text{ (ii)} = \text{xl–xlviii.} \end{array} \right.$

Ez. β   = xxviii–xxxix exclusive of

Ez. ββ   = xxxvi. 24–38.

Ez. α and Ez. β are the work of two collaborators; Ez. ββ is an independent version made for lectionary purposes. The following lists exhibit (1) the main contrasts between Ez. α (i) and Ez. β, (2) renderings common to the two portions of Ez. α, showing that they are the work of a single translator, (3) renderings common to Ez. α and the third book of Reigns, (4) the peculiarities of Ez. ββ with an inquiry into their origin.

(1) *Contrasts between the two main translators.*

	Hebrew	Ezekiel α i (i–xxvii)	Ezekiel β (xxviii–xxxix)
		PHRASES	
1	'(Prophesy and) say' (אמרת)	(προφήτευσον καὶ) ἐρεῖς always to xxvii. 3	(προφήτευσον καὶ) εἰπόν[1] 14 times from xxviii. 12 to xxxix. 1
2	'(They) shall know that I am the Lord' (כי אני יהוה)	{ἐπιγνώσ(ονται) διότι or γνώσ(ονται) ὅτι ἐγὼ Κύριος to xxvi. 6 *passim*	γνώσ(ονται) ὅτι ἐγὼ εἰμι[2] Κύριος from xxviii. 23 (where B has διότι) to xxxix. 28 *passim*
		PLACE NAMES	
3	צור, צר	Σόρ[3] 10 times xxvi–vii	Τύρος xxviii–ix
4	'Tubal and Meshech'	ἡ σύμπασα[4] καὶ τὰ παρατείνοντα xxvii. 13	Μόσοχ καὶ Θοβέλ (with variants) xxxii. 26, xxxviii. 2, xxxix. 1

[1] ἐρεῖς in xxxvii. 4. In α εἰπόν renders the imperat. אמר.

[2] εἰμι is omitted in xxxvi. 38 B (= ββ) and xxxvii. 14.

[3] Only again in Jer. xxi. 13.

[4] = תֵּבֵל (cf. Nah. i. 5). ἡ Ἑλλὰς καὶ ἡ σ. καὶ τὰ π. means apparently 'Greece, both the mainland and the adjoining islands'. Cf. Aristoph. *Nub.* 204 τὴν σύμπασαν (of a map of the world) and just below 212 παρατέταται (of Euboea lying alongside the mainland).

Hebrew	Ezekiel α (i-xxvii)	Ezekiel β (xxviii-xxxix)

GENERAL VOCABULARY

	Hebrew	Ezekiel α (i-xxvii)	Ezekiel β (xxviii-xxxix)
5	אגפים "bands"	οἱ ἀντιλαμβανόμενοι xii. 14 παράταξις xvii. 21	οἱ περί (τινα) xxxviii. 6 bis, 9, xxxix. 4 οἱ μετά (τινος) xxxviii. 22
6	שמם, שממה and cognates	ἀφανίζειν[1] iv. 17, xx. 26, xxv. 3 ἀφανισμός (8 or 9 times)	ἐρημοῦν xxix. 12, &c. (8 times) ἔρημος (10 times) ἐρημία xxxv. 9 ἀπώλεια xxix. 9, 10, 12, xxxii. 15
7	בז, בזז and cognates	διαρπάζειν vii. 21 διαρπαγή xxiii. 46, xxv. 7	σκυλεύειν[2] xxix. 19, xxxviii. 12 f., xxxix. 10 σκῦλον xxix. 19, xxxviii. 12 f.
8	זרה	διασκορπίζειν v. 2, 10, vi. 5 (xx. 23 A) διασπείρειν (v. 12 A) xii. 14 f., xx. 23, xxii. 15 σκορπίζειν v. 12	λικμᾶν xxix. 12, xxx. 23, 26, xxxvi. 19
9	קבץ	εἰσδίχεσθαι xi. 17, xx. 34, 41, xxii. 19, 20 bis	συνάγειν[3] xxviii. 25, &c. (7 times)
10	טוב	καλός[4] xvii. 8, xx. 25, xxiv. 4	ἀγαθός xxxiv. 14 bis (xxxvi. 31 = ββ)
11	דלית, &c.	κλῆμα (5 or 6 times)	κλάδος (6 times)
12	חזק, חזקה	κραταιός iii. 9, 14, xx. 33 f. δυνατός iii. 8	ἰσχυρός[5] xxx. 22, xxxiv. 4, 16
13	גאון	ὑπερηφανία vii. 20, xvi. 49, 56	ὕβρις xxx. 6, 18, xxxii. 12, xxxiii. 28

The β portion has many other peculiarities, e. g. :—

(i) In *prepositions* &c.: the use of ἀντί in causal sense in ἀντὶ τοῦ with inf. (5 times), ἀντὶ τούτου xxviii. 7, xxxiv. 9 ; a larger use of διά with accusative, including διὰ τό (μή) with inf. (Ez. α only in the phrase διὰ τοῦτο) ; εἰ μήν = אם לא in asseverations (5 times ; also v. 11 B, Ez. α else has ἐὰν μή) ; ἡνίκα ἄν xxxii. 9, xxxiii. 33, xxxv. 11 (where α writes ἐν τῷ with inf.) ; περικύκλῳ (10 times ; cf. ὑπερκύκλῳ xxxii. 23 A) ; ὑπό with gen. (3 times ; never in α).

(ii) In *general vocabulary*: δοῦλος = עבד (6 times ; παῖς Ez. xlvi. 17) ; ἐξελέσθαι (α uses ῥύεσθαι, σώζειν) ; καταδουλοῦν, κατεργάζεσθαι, ταράσσειν, &c.

(iii) In *syntax* the practice of placing a dependent genitive

---

[1] Also in ββ (xxxvi. 34 bis, 35 bis, 36) and xxxvi. 4.

[2] Also xxvi. 12. There is some overlapping of the two styles in xxvi-vii.

[3] Also with v. l. ἐπισυνάγειν in xvi. 37 (on this chap. see p. 26) ; ββ has ἀθροίζειν, xxxvi. 24.

[4] Also xxxiv. 18.   [5] Also xxvi. 17 AQ (Hexaplaric).

pronoun (or noun) before its governing noun becomes frequent from the point where the two styles overlap, xxvi. 11 f., xxvii. 11, xxviii. 2, xxxi. 14 = xxxii. 24, xxxii. 20, &c. (Rare in the earlier chapters: v. 11, ix. 10 B).

Of the rarer examples of *agreement* of the α and β portions perhaps the most noteworthy is ἐκκενοῦν μάχαιραν (or ῥομφαίαν) three times in α, twice in β (v. 2, 12, xii. 14; xxviii. 7, xxx. 11), a literal rendering of the Heb. 'empty out' (*i.e.* 'draw') 'the sword', but not without precedent of a kind in late Greek; cf. *Anth. Pal.* vi. 326 ἐκκενοῦν ἰούς = 'to use up all one's arrows'. Other instances are πέλτη (xxiii. 24 and four times in β; not else in LXX) and στηρίζειν τὸ πρόσωπον (α eight times, β thrice; but xxxv. 2 ἐπιστρέφειν τὸ πρόσ.); in xxxvii. 7 two α words occur in close proximity, ἑκάτερος (cf. i. 11 f.) and ἁρμονία (cf. xxiii. 42, in different sense). These and a few other sporadic exx. may be due to chance or to co-operation. Co-operation must, I think, be the cause of the more numerous instances in the first two chapters of β (xxvi f.).

(2) *Renderings common to the two portions of Ezekiel α (absent from β).*

The instances abound, notwithstanding the different subject-matter of the two portions. An asterisk indicates that the word or rendering occurs here only in the LXX.

τὸ αἴθριον (like Lat. *atrium*) ix, x; xl, xlvii

ἀπέναντι i–xxvi; xl, xlii

ἀφηγούμενος (נשׂיא) xi–xxii; xlv ff.

*ἀφορισμός xx. 31, 40; xlviii. 8

*διπλασιάζειν xxi. 14; xliii. 2

ἐγγίζειν vii–xxiii; xl–xlv

εἰσπορεύεσθαι (בוא) viii–xxvi; xlii–xlvi

*ἐνθυμήματα[1] (|| גלולים 'idols') xiv. 5, &c., passim; xliv. 10

ἐχόμενος -ον -α i–xi; xlii–xlviii

ἡγούμενος 5 times in either part

κατά with genit. Pt. i 3 times, Pt. ii 8 times

κατέναντι i, iii, xi; xl–xlvii

*κόλασις (= מכשול) xiv, xviii; xliv

κόμη xxiv. 23; xliv. 20

κορυφή (ראשׁ) Pt. i 3 times; Pt. ii once

τὰ νόμιμα v–xx; xliii–iv

ὃν τρόπον x–xxv; xl–xlviii

ὅρασις and ὄψις

τὸ παράπαν with neg. (no Heb. equivalent) xx. 9, 14 f., 22; xli. 6, xlvi. 20

παραπικραίνων οἶκος α passim; xliv. 6

παρέξ xv. 4; xlii. 14

πρόθυρον (פתח etc.) viii–xi; xliii–xlvii

σαγήνη (חרם)[2] xxvi. 5, 14; xlvii. 10

σκεῦος (כלי)[3] ix–xxvii; xl

συντελεῖν iv–xxiii; xlii f.

τάσσειν (שׂום, שׂים) iv–xxiv; xl–xliv

τρισσός and τρισσῶς

ὑπέρ and ὑπεράνω

ὑπόστασις

Use of the historic pres. in the phrase πίπτω ἐπὶ πρόσωπόν μου ii–xi; xliii f.

[1] Through confusion of the gutturals ⅃ and ע in dictation. The Gr. represents עלילות.

[2] In β ἄγκιστρον (xxxii. 3).

[3] In β ὅπλον (xxxii. 27).

Over against this habitual agreement of the two parts of Ez. α must be set one remarkable instance of apparent discrepancy, in the treatment of the divine title ADONAI JHWH (R. V. 'the Lord God '). The composite name is a special feature of Ezekiel, occurring in the M. T. upwards of 200 times. In cod. B the equivalents in the various portions of the book are as follows:

In α (i) normally Κύριος; rarely κύριος Κύριος (5 exx. only in i–xx, afterwards more frequently).

In β normally κύριος Κύριος; rarely Κύριος.

In ββ ἀδωναὶ Κύριος.

In α (ii) with one exception [1] uniformly Κύριος ὁ θεός (xliii–iv), Κύριος θεός (xlv–end).

Thus α (i) writes Κύριος singly or duplicated; α (ii) Κύριος (ὁ) θεός with or without the article.

The evidence is set out in full in an essay on the Divine Names in Ezekiel, with special reference to the LXX text, contributed by Herr Herrmann to a volume of O. T. studies which appeared in 1913, dedicated to Professor Kittel on his sixtieth birthday.[2] Hermann infers from the above evidence a plurality of translators (probably three) in Ezekiel. His lines of demarcation practically coincide with mine. He places the beginning of the second translator's work 'somewhere about chap. xxvii', noting, as I did, some confusion (*Verwirrung*) of the two styles at the juncture. His third portion begins, like mine, at chap. xl. He differs from me in attributing this portion to a third translator.

Hermann's survey was limited to the Divine Names. He would doubtless have modified his view, had he carried his investigation further. This solitary instance cannot outweigh the numerous examples of agreement between the two portions of Ez. α.

The problem opens up large questions. Divergent renderings of divine titles are commonly an index of a change of translators. This title is, however, peculiar. JHWH was the ineffable Name; AD(O)N(A)I (the other tetragrammaton) was the spoken substitute which eventually superseded it. The hallowing of the Name by means of this surrogate antedates the Greek translators, who constantly render JHWH by Κύριος, the equivalent of ADONAI. What was the import of the combination ADONAI JHWH? Did Ezekiel ever write it and how often? Or is ADONAI in this

---

[1] xliii. 27 Κύριος. On xliii. 18 Κύριος ὁ θεὸς 'Ισραήλ see below.

[2] Professor G. A. Cooke kindly drew my attention to this paper.

connéxion a 'doublet', a mere scribal injunction, 'Pronounce Adonai'? Speaking with diffidence I should venture to share Cornill's opinion that, while the double name was occasionally employed by the prophet himself, the use has been widely extended by his copyists.[1]

The apparent discrepancy in the practice of Ez. α may be variously explained.

The most probable view, in my opinion, is that there is no discrepancy. Translator α in i–xxvii wrote Κύριος, finding יהוה only in his text; in xl–xlviii he found אדני יהוה which he rendered by Κύριος (ὁ) θεός. The inconsistency of practice lies not in the translation but in the original Hebrew. Cod. B, with its rare κ̄ς κ̄ς in the first half of the book, is undoubtedly nearer to the original than the MSS. which keep the double name throughout; but that even B has not escaped interpolation is shown by our earliest witness, the Old Latin of Tyconius, which has a single *Dominus* in passages where B duplicates κ̄ς.

Alternatively, discrepancy in the Greek, if and so far as it exists, might be explained by *pronunciation*. The Massoretic rule that יהוה in conjunction with אדני took the vowel points, not of אדני, but of אלהים, probably rests on earlier practice and would account for the use of (ὁ) θεός in xl–xlviii. The reader who dictated the Hebrew of that portion of the book followed the rule, which was neglected in the portions which employ κ̄ς κ̄ς.

The practice of *abbreviation* in the original Hebrew is a further factor which should not be forgotten. That יהוה was represented by ' is shown by the confusion of the Name with the first personal suffix; e.g. Ez. xxxviii. 20 ἀπὸ προσώπου Κυρίου (‖ 'at *my* presence'), and conversely Jer. vi. 11 τὸν θυμόν μου (‖ 'the fury of JHWH'). But ' might also stand both for Israel (Ez. xlv. 8) and for Judah (xxxvii. 19). Now אדני יהוה is in two instances, one in each part of Ez. α, represented by Κύριος ὁ θεὸς Ἰσραήλ.[2] Ἰσραήλ here doubtless represents a Hebrew '. This suggests the possibility that already in the days of the Greek translation the tetragrammaton might be variously represented by a single, a double, or even a triple *yôd*, which has been erroneously expanded by the translator, and that Adonai formed no part of the original text.

---

[1] Hermann, on the other hand, upholds the originality of the 217 exx. in the M. T.

[2] Ez. iv. 14; xliii. 18 (the first occurrence of the double name in this portion). Also xx. 47 A.

These abbreviations or assumed abbreviations deserve remark. The letter ב was read as בית (Ez. xii. 23, xx. 5), also probably as בני; hence the constant interchange of 'house of Israel' and 'children of Israel'. א was read as אשר (Ez. xlvi. 19).[1] אם לא was expressed by the initial radicals of the two words, which were read as אל, Gr. ἐπί (xxxvi. 7.); Ginsburg quotes a parallel in 2 Kings vi. 27. In Jer. iii. 19 the three radicals of איך 'how' were expanded by the translator into אמן יהוה כי (γένοιτο Κύριος ὅτι).[2]

(3) Renderings common to Ezekiel a and 3 Reigns.

As already stated, the evidence suggesting a common translator for these books is clearest in the sections relating to the two Temples (3 R. vi f.; Ez. xl ff.). The Ezekiel translator might be expected to avail himself of any existing version of the narrative of the earlier Temple. But that this is no mere case of imitation appears from the parallels scattered over other parts of the two books. An asterisk indicates that the Greek word or rendering occurs in the LXX only in the passages cited; a dagger that the word is not used elsewhere in the Books of Reigns.

	Hebrew		3 Reigns	Ezekiel a
		Description of Temple (vi f.)		
1	אולם	†αἰλάμ	vi. 7, &c.	viii. 16; xl-xlvi
2	Misc.	†γεῖσος	vii. 46	xl-xliii
3	Misc.	†γραφίς	vi. 28	xxiii. 14
4	Misc.	†διάστημα	vi. 11, vii. 46	xli-xlviii
5	Misc.	†διάταξις (architectural term)	vi. 5, 14 A	xlii f.
6	Doubtful	†ἔνδεσμος (archit.)	vi. 15	xiii. 11
7	Doubtful	*ζυγοῦν (ἐζυγωμένα)	vii. 43	xli. 26
8	*κρ. = אטם	*θυρίδες κρυπταί	vi. 9	xl. 16, xli. 26
9	*פתח =	θύρωμα	vi. 30, vii. 42	xl-xlii
10	גב	νῶτος *(of felloe of a wheel)	vii. 19	i. 18, x. 12
11	אחור	†τὰ ὀπίσθια	vii. 13	viii. 16
12	סף	πρόθυρον	vii. 36	xliii. 8 [3]
13	Misc.	*στοά	vi. 31	xl. 18, xlii. 3, 5
14	Misc.	τρισσῶς	vii. 41 f.	xli. 16 (xvi. 30)
15	(שלישי)	†τὰ τριώροφα [4]	vi. 13	xli. 7 (M. T. different)
16	(סבן)	*φατνοῦν	vii. 40	xli. 15 (M.T. different)

[1] τῶν ἱερέων = אשר לב' (for אל הכ').   [2] I owe this instance to Duhm.

[3] Redpath gives a wrong Hebrew equivalent here.

[4] Word else only in Gen. vi. 16.

	Hebrew		3 Reigns	Ezekiel α
			In other parts of the book.	
17	כלי	†ἄγγος	xvii. 10	iv. 9
18	*נשא =	†ἀντιλαμβάνεσθαι	ix. 11 [cf. 9]	xx. 5 f.
19	Misc.	†ἀπερείδεσθαι	xiv. 28	xxiv. 2
20	אלה	†ἀρά	viii. 31	xvii. 13, 16
21	שפט	†διακρίνειν	iii 9	xx. 35 f., xliv. 24[1]
22	Misc.	†δράξ	xvii. 12	x. 2, xiii. 19
23	Misc.	†ἐκποιεῖν	ςxi. 10	xlvi. 7, 11
24	נפח ,פוח	†ἐμφυσᾶν	xvii. 21	xxi. 31 (xxii. 20 A)[2]
25	שלח	†ἐπαποστέλλειν	xii. 24 kB	xiv. 19 (21 A)
26	*גלולים‖ ('idols')	†ἐπιτηδεύματα[3]	xv. 12	vi. 9, xiv. 6, xx. 7 f., 18, 39
27	Misc.	*κατ᾽ εὐθύ	xxi. 23, 25	xlvi. 9
28	תא	*τὸ θεέ	xiv. 28	xl. 7 ff.
29	רב	†ἱκανούσθω	xii. 28, xix. 4, xxi. 11	xliv. 6, xlv. 9
30	Doubtful	*καινότης	viii. 53	xlvii. 12
31	חדר	κοιτών	xxi. 30	viii. 12
32	Misc.	†λάλημα	ix. 7	xxiii. 10[4]
33	No equivalent	†τὸ παράπαν	xi. 10	xx. 9, &c., xli. 6, xlvi. 20
34	מרה ,מרי	†παραπικραίνειν	xiii. 21, 26	*passim*
35	Misc.	παρέξ	iii. 18, xii. 20	xv. 4, xlii. 14
36	חל	προτείχισμα	xx. 23	[xl. 5 = *al.*], xlii. 20, xlviii. 15
37	רענן	†σύσκιος	xiv. 23 (ὑποκάτω ξύλου σ.)	vi. 13 (ὑποκάτω δένδρου σ.)[5]
38	עליון	ὑψηλός	ix. 8	ix. 2
39	Misc.	†χάραξ	xii. 24 fB, xxi. 12 *bis*	iv. 2, xxi. 22 *bis*, xxvi. 8

(4) *Ezekiel* ββ (= xxxvi. 24–38) *a version made for lectionary use.*

Beside the broad lines of demarcation between Ez. α and Ez. β, the above passage, of fifteen verses, stands apart and cannot be attributed to either translator. It falls within the province of β but has no kinship with his work. It contains the promise of Israel's restoration to their own land, their 'baptism' from past impurities, the removal of the old stony

---

[1] Also twice in Ez. β (xxxiv. 17, 20).

[2] Also in Ez. β (xxxvii. 9).

[3] = עלילות ('practices'). Error due to confusion of gutturals in dictation; cf. ἐνθυμήματα in List (2) above, p. 120.

[4] Also Ez. xxxvi. 3; and once only elsewhere in LXX.

[5] Else only Cant. i. 16.

heart and the gift of the spirit of God; and, along with this spiritual renewal, promises of the material blessings of rich harvests, a cultivated land, waste cities rebuilt, and a population comparable in number with the sacrificial flocks at the festivals.

Now the Greek of this passage stands out prominently from its context; it is a patch of a different texture from the surrounding fabric. The limits can be exactly defined. It is bounded on either side by one of the characteristic marks of translator β, viz. the presence of εἰμι in the phrase 'shall know that I am the LORD' (xxxvi. 23, xxxvii. 6), while within the section the auxiliary is omitted (vv. 36, 38 B text). In this instance ββ is at one with α; elsewhere it diverges from the style of both translators and recalls the manner of the Asiatic school, Theodotion in particular. The peculiarities are as follows:—

v. 24 ἀθροίσω. The Heb. verb (קבץ piel) is rendered in a by εἰσδέχεσθαι (five times), in β by συνάγειν [1] (seven times). Ἀθροίζειν, here only in Ez. LXX, is the rendering of Theodotion in this book (xx. 34) and elsewhere.

ib. γαιῶν (ארצות). Biblical translators as a rule avoid the rare plural of γῆ. The substitute employed by our pair of translators and others is χῶραι. The poetical γαῖαι, here only in Ez. LXX, was preferred by the Asiatic school and is used by 'the three' in Ez. xxix. 12.

v. 31 προσοχθιεῖτε κατὰ πρόσωπον αὐτῶν (Heb. 'ye shall loathe yourselves in your own sight'). Προσοχθίζειν here only in Ez. Translator a writes κόπτεσθαι (τὰ) πρόσωπα (vi. 9, xx. 43); but Theod. in the first passage has the same phrase as here and in the second a similar one, with the same confusion of persons.[2]

v. 32 ff. The outstanding peculiarity in ββ is the use of the transliteration ἀδωναί before Κύριος in the B text, in vv. 33 and 37 in the first hand, in v. 32 in the hands of both correctors, where the first hand wrote κύριος Κύριος, the ordinary equivalent in β of ADONAI JHWH. The transliteration in v. 33 has the support of the Old Latin of Tyconius (ed. Burkitt, Texts and Studies, iii, p. 33; in v. 32 the Lat. has Dominus only, the quotation does not extend to v. 37). Only once again in the LXX does ἀδωναί appear in cod. B, viz. in the Prayer of Hannah (1 R. i. 11), the original Haphtarah for New Year's Day. Ἀδωναὶ Κύριος is the rendering of the Asiatic school.

v. 34 ἀνθ' ὧν ὅτι = תחת אשר, ordinarily rendered in Ez. by ἀνθ' ὧν. Such combinations of particles are characteristic of the Asiatic school. This one recurs in the LXX only in the later portions of the Books of Reigns (App. I. 4) and in Deut. xxviii. 62; Theod. has it twice in Jeremiah.

ib. παροδεύοντος. The Gk. verb, here only in the translated books of the LXX, similarly renders עבר in Symmachus (Ez. xxxiii. 28). Ez. a employs διοδεύειν (v. 14, xiv. 15) and, in common with Ez. β, διαπορεύεσθαι.

[1] Also in xvi. 37.
[2] Unless we should read αὐτῶν = ὑμῶν αὐτῶν.

v. 35 ὡς κῆπος τρυφῆς. Here only in LXX is κῆπος used of the garden of Eden; the normal παράδεισος appears four times in β (xxviii. 13, xxxi. 8 f.); but Theod. has κῆπος in those passages and in Genesis. The O.L. of Tyconius attests this reading (hortus).

Lastly in vv. 36, 38, as already mentioned, the εἰμι which translator β regularly inserts in the prophet's refrain is here omitted in the best MSS.

The abnormalities of this section are not confined to the Greek. The M. T. itself has one grammatical peculiarity requiring explanation, viz. the solitary instance in this book of the longer form of the 1st pers. pron. ānokī (v. 28), whereas ănī occurs 138 times (Brown-Driver-Briggs, Heb. Lex. s. v.). Another pronominal ἅπαξ λεγόμενον appears in v. 35, the fem. form הלזו.

It occurred to me that the peculiarities of this isolated section might have a *lectionary* explanation. Alike in subject-matter and in length it was adapted for public reading; and, in fact, I found ancient authority for such use in both Christian and Jewish services. Two questions then arose. (1) Has this Greek lesson come to us from Church or Synagogue? (2) Is it earlier or later than its context?

(1) Is it a Christian lesson? In the scheme of O. T. lessons in use in the Greek Church, preserved in LXX lectionaries, the first five verses of our passage are assigned to the vigil (παραμονή) of Pentecost; and the whole passage, lacking the first verse, still stands in our English lectionary as an alternative lesson for the evening of Whit-Sunday. The promise of the Spirit in v. 27 explains the selection. On the other hand the version is obviously Jewish, the product of the Palestinian-Asiatic school of translators. Its peculiarities, as was seen, appear already in the Old Latin (probably second century) version used by Tyconius. It is hard to believe that at that early date a Christian lesson had such far-reaching influence as to affect all known MSS. and to leave no trace of any earlier version. We must, I think, go further back and seek the explanation in the synagogue worship.

With the Jews our passage was the primitive *Haphtarah* for the sabbath known as that of the 'Red Cow'.[1] The lesson seems to have been originally confined to v. 25; that verse, 'I will sprinkle clean water upon you and ye shall be clean', gave the passage its special appropriateness for the Jewish sabbath, as v. 27 for the Christian Pentecost. If the choice of a festival

---

[1] פרה אדמה Num. xix. 2; the R. V. rendering 'red heifer' seems to be unwarranted. On this sabbath see Dr. Büchler's articles in J. Q. R. v. 427, 448 ff., vi. 6 ff.

important enough profoundly to affect the Greek text lies between Pentecost and Red Cow Sabbath, one might be tempted to give precedence to the former. In reality, the Red Cow leads us right back to the origins of the Jewish lectionary. The sabbath takes its name from the nineteenth chapter of the Book of Numbers, containing the law of purification from pollution by the use of a liquid in which the main ingredient consisted of the ashes of a red cow. The medicated waters were laid aside for the removal of impurity as 'water of sprinkling'.

I am not concerned with the origin of a practice which the Priestly Code doubtless took over from paganism; merely with the use to which the narrative was put in the Jewish liturgy. 'Red Cow (or *Parah*) Sabbath' was one of four 'extraordinary' sabbaths, which in Talmudic times fell in the last month of the ecclesiastical year.[1] The sabbaths were extraordinary in that there were allocated to them special lessons, from which they took their names, falling outside the ordinary course of Pentateuch readings. The sabbaths and lessons were as follows:—

Sabbath	First lesson	Second lesson
1 *Shekalim*, 'Shekels'	Ex. xxx. 11 ff. (the half shekel tax)	2 K. xii (contributions for Temple repairs) *or* 2 Ez. xlv. 12 (value of the shekel)
2 *Zakor*, 'Remember (Amalek)'	Deut. xxv. 17 ff.	1 Sam. xv (Saul and Amalekites)
3 *Parah*, '(Red) Cow'	Num. xix	Ez. xxxvi. 25
4 *Hahodesh*, 'The month'	Ex. xii. 1 ff. ('This month shall be unto you', &c.)	Ez. xlv. 18 (cleansing of sanctuary on New Year's Day)

It has been established beyond doubt that the practice of sabbath readings began with the above four passages from the Pentateuch. Not only did they supersede the ordinary cycle lessons, but Jewish tradition, which recognizes distinct stages in lectionary development, assigns these particular lessons to the earliest stage. If the ordinary sabbath readings were the institution of Ezra, the lessons for the special sabbaths and the festivals were ascribed to no less a person than the lawgiver.[3]

[1] See the Jewish Calendar in Appendix V.
[2] According to Karaite tradition.
[3] *J. Q. R.* v. 426, quoting *Sopherim* xxi. 4.

The statement, exaggerated as it is, witnesses to a belief in the remote antiquity of a custom of which the origin was forgotten. That origin has been reconstructed with great probability by Dr. Büchler. He maintains that the practice of Torah readings on the festivals and special sabbaths originated in controversy on disputed points of ritual. Of the four special lessons three deal with eminently contentious topics : the Temple half shekel, the red cow (both these are the subjects of special treatises in the Talmud), the fixing of New Year's Day. Again, there are indications that the allocation of these four lessons to the last month of the year was not the original one, and that they were transposed to the end of the calendar when the triennial cycle was introduced. Another tradition connects the 'Red Cow'° with the beginning of Nisan, not with the end of Adar, from which Dr. Büchler infers that there was a time when this passage 'formed the scriptural lesson for *the first sabbath in Nisan*'.[1] If he is right, the lesson acquires greater importance ; it was a call to purification on the opening sabbath of the new year.

Passing from the first to the second lesson, here again we find evidence that the *Haphtaroth* for the special sabbaths were introduced before those for the ordinary sabbaths, perhaps even before the festival lessons. It will be observed that, according to one tradition, three out of the four were drawn from Ezekiel. From this and other circumstances Dr. Büchler regards it as a 'certain conclusion that the earliest Haftaras were taken from this book, and were originally assigned to the festivals and special sabbaths'.[2]

Reverting to Ez. xxxvi, the document to which one naturally turns to discover whether the lectionary use may have influenced the text is the Targum, the Aramaic paraphrase read in the Palestinian synagogues. The Targum[3] quotes *v.* 25 in the following form : 'And I will forgive your sins, *even as they are cleansed with the water of sprinkling and with the ashes of the cow of the sin-offering*; and ye shall be cleansed from all your impurities', &c. The second lesson is here interpreted in the light of the first. Again the concluding verse (38) runs : 'As the holy people, *as the people which is purified and comes to Jerusalem at the time of the solemn assemblies of Passover*, so shall the desolate cities of Israel be full of men', &c. Ezekiel

---

[1] *J. Q. R.* v. 449.   [2] *ib.* vi. 7.   [3] I use Walton's Polyglott.

specifies no particular feast; the Targum associates the passage with a lustration at the opening year in preparation for Passover. These extracts show how closely this section was linked with the sabbath of the Red Cow. I have little doubt that the idio-syncrasies of the Greek text have a similar lectionary origin.

(2) Is Ezekiel ββ earlier or later than its context? The answer to this question is not so easy as it seems. It is difficult to understand how a later version could so completely supersede that of the original company; that the Alexandrians incorporated a lectionary version already current in Palestine is quite in-telligible. On the other hand, the style unquestionably favours the second alternative. The marks of the ' Palestinian-Asiatic ' school are obvious. A mere transliteration like ἀδωναί is not necessarily ' a Hexaplaric interpolation ' as Cornill holds.[1] Trans-literation of divine names sometimes preceded translation; σαβαώθ is retained in the first book of Reigns and Isaiah where later translators wrote παντοκράτωρ. Ἀδωναί curiously reappears in cod. B only in another old Jewish lesson (1 R. i. 11); for public reading it may have been customary to preserve the Hebrew form. But the accumulation of unusual renderings clearly indicates non-Egyptian origin; and, though the Asiatic school apparently arose before the time of Aquila,[2] we have no ground for carrying its beginnings back to so early a date as the second or first century B.C. The phenomena resemble those presented by the Books of Reigns, the unedifying parts of which were filled in by *Asiaticus*; with the difference that here we have, not a passage which there was any reason to expunge, but one which would be among the first to call for translation. On the whole, I can only suppose that, in some unexplained way, early in our era a later version of this lectionary passage supplanted that of the original Alexandrian company in the parent MS. from which all our MSS. are descended.

[1] *Das Buch des Proph. Ez.* (1886), p. 173.
[2] See p. 26 above.

APPENDIX IV

THE BISECTION OF OLD TESTAMENT BOOKS

It was shown, that the Greek translators of Jeremiah and Ezekiel divided either book into two approximately equal parts, unless indeed they merely took over this mechanical division from their Hebrew exemplar. But this practice of bipartition is not peculiar to these two books. I propose to collect here (1) some further internal evidence afforded by other LXX books, (2) the external evidence, of a rather miscellaneous character, for the prevalence of this custom of bisection.

Internal evidence. I can quote no further examples for bisection on the part of the *translators.* I can, however, point to a similar bipartition on the part of the *scribes* of the parent MSS. from which all our oldest uncials are descended, in the case of no less than three books, Exodus, Leviticus, and the Psalter.[1] The differences between the two halves are here purely orthographical. Their importance lies in their witness to a practice of copyists, at a date far earlier than that of our oldest MSS., of dividing the books into two nearly equal portions. The uncials have, in these orthographical details, faithfully transmitted to us the varieties in spelling of an earlier age and given us an insight into the form of the archetypes.

In Exodus and Leviticus I have detected one certain clue only ; but, if it stands alone, it is shared by both books, and the coincidence cannot be accidental. It consists in the use or disuse of the form ἐάν for ἄν after the relative pronoun ὅς or after a conjunction (ἡνίκα). I follow the B text, but the other uncials give much the same result. In the first half of both books. ὃς ἄν and ὃς ἐάν are used interchangeably ; in the latter half of Exodus ὃς ἄν is universal, in the corresponding part of Leviticus nearly universal. The break in Exodus falls at about xxiii. 20, in Leviticus at or near the end of chap. xv.[2]

---

[1] The evidence is given more fully in an article in the *J. T. S.* vol. ix, pp. 88-98.

[2] The papyri show that the classical ὃς ἄν was normal till towards the end of the second century B. C., when ὃς ἐάν came in and remained thenceforth the predominant form.

In the Psalter the clues are more numerous; the division clearly occurs at the end of Ψ. lxxvii LXX (lxxviii Heb.). Though mere itacisms and the like, they are very significant. (1) Down to the end of Ψ. lxxvii the uncials, with few exceptions, write feminine nouns in -εία (or -εια) without an epsilon, δυναστία, εὐπρέπια, μεγαλοπρέπια and the like; after that point they employ the normal spelling. (2) In the B text αι and ε are constantly interchanged in Part I, the last instance of this itacism occurring in Ψ. lxxvii. 12, παιδίῳ for πεδίῳ. (3) In Part I the uncials insert the augment in the past tenses of εὐφραίνειν, in Part II they omit it.[1]

A second line of inquiry leads to a similar conclusion. In some minuscules the *character of the text* changes in the middle of a book; from that point onwards the MS. joins another group or family of MSS. I have been at the pains to trace throughout the several books of the Pentateuch, in the larger Cambridge Septuagint, the relationship of the text of each document to that of codex B, which may for this purpose be regarded as constant. Such an investigation of 'the allies of B' clearly brings out the lack of homogeneity in certain MSS.; the type of text in one and the same MS. is found to vary from book to book. Originally the constituent books of the Pentateuch must have been written on separate rolls, and MSS. which exhibit one type of text (say) in Exodus and another in Leviticus witness to their descent from archetypes so written. But in a few minuscules the change occurs in the *middle* of a book. An interesting 'variable' of this kind is the Paris Cod. o of Brooke and McLean (= 82 of Holmes and Parsons). In Genesis its text is Hexaplaric; throughout Exodus, and in the latter half of Numbers, it is one of B's strongest supporters; in the rest of the Pentateuch, including the first half of Numbers, it goes with the multitude against B; in the Books of Reigns it joins the Lucianic group. In Numbers the change occurs at xvii. 10 LXX, which is almost exactly the middle point; according to the Massoretic reckoning the middle verse fell five verses earlier.[2]

Thus internal evidence of three distinct kinds—style, orthography, type of text—indicates that the 'half-book' was a recognized unit alike for translators and for copyists of primitive LXX

---

[1] It may be accidental that in a Psalter in the Library of Caius College, Cambridge (H. and P. 206), the Psalm titles are wanting after Ψ. lxxvi.

[2] Similar phenomena occur in cod. a (Exodus and Leviticus) and cod. h (Exodus and Joshua).

MSS. It will be observed that each of the three divisions of the Hebrew Bible is represented: Pentateuch (three books), Prophets (two), Psalter. This widespread recurrence of a break of one kind or another at the midway point cannot be fortuitous.

External evidence. Before I quote the Hebrew witnesses, a few passages in classical authors deserve remark. It would appear that the custom of dividing a work into two halves was not uncommon with authors and editors in the ancient world at large. The physician Galen, in a eulogy on his master Hippocrates, commends him for not, like others, writing books of 10,000 words (or lines), to be afterwards cut up by their author into two: 'libros scribens decem milium verborum (or "versuum"), deinde ipse rursum *dividens eos bifariam ut alteruter sit per se.*' Dr. Birt, to whose *Die Buchrolle in der Kunst*[1] I owe the reference, has more to say on this practice of Greek authors; he thinks that Thucydides' History was originally written in two rolls, of which the second began at V. 26 with a renewed claim to authorship, γέγραφε δὲ καὶ ταῦτα ὁ αὐτὸς Θουκυδίδης Ἀθηναῖος. Aulus Gellius quotes Varro on a linguistic point to the effect that a book divided into two equal parts should be described not as *dimidium* but as *dimidiatum librum.*[2]

But it is Hebrew practice with which I am directly concerned. And here, I think, we must distinguish (though the two things may have a common origin) between authors' practice and scribes' practice—between the division of a work by its author or redactor into approximately equal portions with distinct subject-matter and a more mechanical bisection on the part of later copyists.

An instance of the former class is found, as already stated,[3] in Ezekiel, half Desolation, half Consolation. Joshua is another, with twelve chapters devoted to the conquest and twelve to the allocation of the conquered territory. In the New Testament we have the two treatises of St. Luke of equal length, while the Acts again falls into two nearly equal parts.

Then there are examples which seem to fall between the two types. In the Books of Samuel, Kings, and Chronicles, we have three concrete instances of the subdivision of a book originally single. Here the partitionists (apparently the Greek translators) seem to have been guided partly by subject-matter, partly by regard to proportion. 1 Samuel breaks off approximately at the death of Saul, but there is no obvious reason, other than a

---

[1] Leipzig, 1907, p. 215.   [2] *Noctes Atticae*, iii. 14.   [3] p. 37.

mechanical one, for the dividing-line in the Book of Kings. In both Samuel and Kings the same rule holds good as in all the instances of bisection which I have noted in the LXX, viz. that Book I is slightly longer than Book II. In Chronicles the division (at the death of David) is obviously one of subject-matter. Here the rule is broken; Book II is considerably the longer of the two.

External evidence proving the existence of the practice of mechanical bisection of books is afforded by two important Rabbinical passages.

The first occurs in the tractate *Megilla* of the Jerusalem Talmud.[1] Among other regulations for the guidance of copyists of Scripture the following is laid down: 'The writing on skin (*Gewil*, גויל) should be on the hairy side, on parchment (*Ķelaf*, קלף) on the smooth side; to reverse this arrangement is forbidden. One must not write half of it [i.e. half the book] on skin and half of it on parchment; but one may write one half of it on the skin of a clean tame animal (בהמה) and the other half on the skin of a clean wild animal (חיה).' The passage presupposes a practice of writing either half of a book on different materials.

The second passage occurs in the tractate *Sopherim*.[2] After stating that a copy of the complete Pentateuch must not be split up into its component books, because one must not diminish the sanctity of the whole which is greater than that of its parts, the writer proceeds to mention the reverse process of building up a Pentateuch out of smaller units. 'They do not', he writes, ' combine two books of the Pentateuch [lit. " two-fifths "] into one, *nor a book and a half into one volume*; but if it is intended to add the remainder [i.e. to make up a complete Pentateuch later on] it is permitted.' Here again we have the half-book mentioned as a normal unit. These two passages seem conclusive.[3]

Another piece of evidence, perhaps the most important of all, remains to be mentioned. The Massoretes, among other laborious

---

[1] T. J. *Meg.* 71 a.   I owe the reference to L. Blau, *Studien zum althebräischen Buchwesen* (1902), p. 22.

[2] iii. 4.

[3] The relevance of a third is doubtful. In the Babylonian Talmud (*Baba Bathra*, 13 b) there is a discussion about the division of property between heirs. The Mishna forbids such persons to divide a copy of the Scriptures, on which R. Samuel remarks that this prohibition applies only to a case where the Scriptures are in one roll; if in two, the heirs are at liberty to take one each. But the reference here is apparently to a two volume copy of the whole Old Testament, not to any single book.

calculations, ascertained which was the middle verse, the middle
word, the middle letter in each book of Scripture.   But the
beginnings of this practice date back behind the Massoretes.
In a passage in the Talmud,[1] which cannot be later than A.D. 300,
the custom is already described as ancient.   'The ancients', we
there read, 'were called *Soferim* because they counted all the
letters in the Law.   They said that the *Vav* in the word *gahon*
[Lev. xi. 42] is the middle letter in the Law : the words "diligently
sought" [*ib.* x. 16] the middle words : the verse "then shall he be
shaven" [*ib.* xiii. 33] the middle verse.   The *Ayin* in the word
yâʻar ["wood",Ψ. lxxx. 14(13)] is the middle [letter] in the Psalter,
the verse "But he, being full of compassion, forgave their
iniquity" [Ψ. lxxviii. 38] the middle verse.'   We are not, indeed,
told that the ancients, like the Massoretes, calculated the middle
point in *each book* of the Pentateuch ; but it is noteworthy that
only the Pentateuch and the Psalter are mentioned.   From this
and from the further fact that only in these portions of Scripture
is the middle letter indicated in the M. T. by larger script,
Dr. Ludwig Blau in his 'Massoretic Studies'[2] infers that the
process of calculation began with the law-book and the hymn-
book of the Jewish Church.   And it is just in these portions that
the changes in the orthography of the LXX MSS. occur,
which point to a practice of bisection.

Since the Massoretes based their calculations on earlier models,
we are led to compare their division of the books, according to
verses, with that of the early scribes and translators of the LXX,
and to inquire whether there is any connexion between the two.
The relation, in fact, is practically constant.   *In each book the
Greeks drew their line a little later than the Massoretes.*   In Exodus
the Massoretic division comes at xxii. 27 [28 LXX], that of the
Greek copyists at xxiii. 20, twenty-three verses later ; in Leviticus
the Massoretic Part II begins at xv. 7, the Greek at or about xvi. 1,
twenty-seven verses later ; in Numbers the Massoretic middle point
falls at xvii. 20 [5 LXX], that of the Greeks, as attested by the
variation in the character of the text represented by cod. o (see
above), at xvii. 25 [10 LXX], five verses later.   The Massoretes
bisect the Psalter at lxxviii. 36, 'the ancients' two verses later,
the Greeks at the end of the same Psalm.   In Ezekiel the
Massoretic dividing-line falls at xxvi. 1, the Greek at xxviii. 1,
while throughout this interval of two chapters there is a significant

---

[1] T. B. *Kiddushin*, 30 a.
[2] *J. Q. R.* viii. (1896) and ix. (1897).

mixture of the two styles in the Greek, suggestive of co-operation between the translators. In Jeremiah, owing to the dislocation of text and uncertainty as to the limits of the Greek Part II, no exact comparison is possible. Similarly, as we saw, the Books of Samuel and Kings were broken *a little after* the half-way point.

Can we account for this relation between the two dividing-lines? The middle verse would rarely, if ever, coincide with a break in the subject-matter. Scribes or translators, desiring to approximate as nearly as possible to an equal division, were likely to break the text at *the first convenient halting-place after the central point*. And here we may, I think, push the comparison with the Massoretic procedure a little further. In Exodus the respective dividing-lines are xxii. 27 and xxiii. 20; at xxiii. 20 in the M. T. occurs the first ם after the middle point, the first indication, that is, of the beginning of a new 'open section'— a section for which a new line was required. Similarly at Numbers xvii. 25 (the Greek dividing-line) occurs the first mark of a new section (ם) after the middle point (xvii. 20). In Leviticus one ם intervenes before the transitional point in the Greek, but at that point occurs the first of the larger Massoretic divisions, marked by a triple ם. 'The Psalms', writes Dr. Ginsburg,[1] 'have no sections, as each Psalm constitutes a continuous and undivided whole'; the Greek scribes made their break at the close of the very Psalm which, according to the Massoretes, contained the middle verse.

That the Massoretic practice may have had its counterpart at Alexandria was suggested a quarter of a century ago in Dr. Blau's 'Massoretic Studies' already mentioned. After referring to kindred phenomena in the stichometries of Greek and Latin Bibles, he proceeds : 'I should merely like to suggest the question whether the letter-counting of the Hebrew Bible did not give the students and copyists of the Septuagint the first impulse towards a similar proceeding. The Greek translators and the first people to use and disseminate this version were, of course, Jews, and the possibility that the Greek text of the Bible had its Massoretes as well as the Hebrew is, therefore, not *a priori* to be rejected.'[2] The suggestion, I venture to think, receives remarkable support from the LXX evidence, of which the writer was unaware. Dr. Blau conjectures that, as 'the Grecian stichometry and consequently also the counting of the letters which was connected

---

[1] *Introduction to Heb. Bible*, p. 17.
[2] *J. Q. R.* viii. (1896), p. 355 f.

with it, goes back to the habits of the booksellers of classical antiquity, who paid the copyists on a scale of this sort', so the fixing of the transcribers' remuneration may have given rise to these elaborate Jewish calculations.

Two further testimonies of doubtful import—in art and in tradition—may be appended. For a possible contribution of art to this inquiry reference may be made to the 'double rolls' and 'split rolls' which figure in mediaeval illustrations and are a source of perplexity to Dr. Birt.[1] More apposite, perhaps, is one item, with an apparently underlying element of truth, in a fantastic account of the translation of the Greek Bible by a writer not famous for veracity. Epiphanius, who quotes tradition as his authority (ὡς ᾄδεται λόγος), asserts that the translators were locked up in skylighted cells *in pairs* with attendants and short-hand writers ; each pair was entrusted with one book, the books were then circulated and, in the result, thirty-six identical versions of the whole Bible were produced. Ζυγὴ ζυγὴ κατὰ οἰκίσκον ('a pair to a cell') are his words; and again ἑκάστῃ δὲ ζυγῇ βίβλος μία ἐπεδίδοτο, ὡς εἰπεῖν ἡ βίβλος τῆς τοῦ κόσμου Γενέσεως μιᾷ ζυγῇ, ἡ Ἔξοδος τῶν υἱῶν Ἰσραὴλ τῇ ἄλλῃ ζυγῇ, (τὸ) Λευιτικὸν τῇ ἄλλῃ καὶ καθεξῆς ἄλλη βίβλος τῇ ἄλλῃ.[2] This appears to describe fairly accurately the procedure adopted by the translators of Jeremiah and Ezekiel; in other books internal evidence indicates no more than co-operation of a pair of copyists.

---

[1] *Die Buchrolle in der Kunst,* p. 326, &c.
[2] *De mens. et pond.* 3 ff.

JEWISH CALENDAR

E months are lunar months. The calendar was adapted to the solar year by an occasional intercalary month (a second Adar)

Month	Day	Event
(I) NISAN	1	Ecclesiastical New Year
	14 to 21	{ FEAST OF PASSOVER AND UNLEAVENED BREAD (MAṢṢOTH)
(II) IYYAR		
(III) SIWAN	c. 6	FEAST OF PENTECOST OR WEEKS (SHABUOTH)
(IV) TAMMUZ	17	FAST (BABYL^N CAPTURE OF JERUSALEM) First sabbath of Punishment / Second " / Third "
(V) AB	9	FAST (BURNING OF TEMPLE) First sabbath of Consolation / Second " / Third "
(VI) ELUL	1	New Year for tithes / Fourth sabbath of Consolation / Fifth " / Sixth " / Seventh "

AUTUMN QUARTER

Month	Day	Event
(VII) TISHRI	1	Civil New Year (ROSH HA-SHANAH)
	3	FAST OF GEDALIAH
	10	DAY OF ATONEMENT (YOM KIPPUR)
	15 to 22	{ FEAST OF TABERNACLES (SUKKOTH) AND OF EIGHTH DAY
(VIII) MARḤESHWAN		
(IX) KISLEW	25 to	{ FEAST OF

WINTER QUARTER

Month	Day	Event
(X) TEBETH	2	DEDICATION (ḤANUKKAH)
	10	FAST (BEGINNING OF BABYLONIAN SIEGE OF JERUSALEM)
(XI) SHEBAT		
(XII) ADAR	14 15	Sabbath Shekalim / Sabbath Zakor / { FEAST OF PURIM / Sabbath Parah / Sabbath Ḥaḥodesh

GENERAL INDEX

INDEX OF BIBLICAL AND RABBINICAL REFERENCES

¹ English numeration, with that of LXX in brackets.